Gotthilf Heinrich von Schubert

Explanatory Text to S.R. Urbino's Charts of the Animal Kingdom

Gotthilf Heinrich von Schubert

Explanatory Text to S.R. Urbino's Charts of the Animal Kingdom

ISBN/EAN: 9783337246105

Printed in Europe, USA, Canada, Australia, Japan

Cover: Foto ©ninafisch / pixelio.de

More available books at **www.hansebooks.com**

EXPLANATORY TEXT

TO

S. R. URBINO'S

CHARTS OF THE ANIMAL KINGDOM.

REVISED AND CORRECTED BY

SAMUEL KNEELAND, A.M., M.D.,

INSTRUCTOR IN ZOÖLOGY IN THE MASSACHUSETTS INSTITUTE OF TECHNOLOGY.

BOSTON:
S. R. URBINO, 14 BROMFIELD STREET.
1869.

Entered according to Act of Congress, in the year 1869, by
S. R. URBINO,
in the Clerk's Office of the District Court of the District of Massachusetts.

CAMBRIDGE :
PRESS OF JOHN WILSON AND SON.

DEDICATION.

This work is respectfully dedicated to teachers and students throughout the land, in the hope and in the belief that it will be of assistance to them in the pursuit of one of the most fascinating, useful, and elevating branches of human knowledge.

PREFACE.

The engravings of animals, to which these pages are the accompanying text, may be regarded as an attempt to introduce into common-school education a new feature; viz., the study of natural history.

The most distinguished educators of the day are of one mind as to the great advantages to be derived from a knowledge of the forms and relations of the animal kingdom, as one of the elements in a general education.

The beauty of the objects thus presented to the youthful mind is no small inducement for its early presentation. The varied colors of shells, the glistening hues of insects, and the gorgeous plumage of birds, as simple objects of beauty, cannot fail to interest young persons, and to lay the foundation for a love and appreciation of the beautiful in nature, and in art, the copier of nature.

The study of natural history also sharpens the perceptive faculties, and develops a method and precision in the pursuit of knowledge, which will exert great influence in every sphere of life.

If to this be added the insight into the plan of creation, which an acquaintance with the wonderful adaptation of means to ends (everywhere seen in the animal kingdom) of necessity gives to the student, we feel that no further evidence need be presented of the utility of this study.

The present work is offered with the view of facilitating the teaching and acquiring the principles of natural history. The accuracy, beauty, and artistic representations of the animals on the plates will surely arrest and please the eye, which is the first great step in the natural system of object-teaching.

This is an attempt to popularize the knowledge of natural history, by presenting, in a cheap but scientific form, lifelike pictures of a sufficient number of characteristic animals to show the principal links in the chain of nature.

Of course, it is impossible in a work of this kind to enter minutely into the description of animals and their habits: it is only hoped, in this, to secure the attention of youthful students, and thus so to interest them in the study of natural history, that they will be induced to pursue it in larger works specially intended for the purpose.

S. K.

BOSTON, January, 1869.

CONTENTS.

Mammals 1
Birds 50
Serpents and other Reptiles 94
Fishes 105
   Mollusks 125
Insects 133
   Crustaceans 152
   Worms 153
   Radiates 155

MAMMALIA.

PLATE 1.

MONKEYS.—I. The Orangs and Chimpanzee (*Simia*) are those which resemble man the most: their head is round; their eyes and ears, although small, are constructed after the human type; their face, as well as breast, is hairless; they have no tail, &c., as most other monkeys have. When standing upright, they are about as tall as a middle-sized man.

They inhabit the warmest parts of Asia, Africa, and Oceanica.

a. The CHIMPANZEE (*Simia Troglodytes*) (*Troglodytes niger*) has long been known, and always considered as a very intelligent and mild ape. All Natural Historians, who have had an opportunity of observing it in confinement, praise it for its amiableness and intelligence. Only language is wanting to make it a more preferable companion for man than any other animal.

The Chimpanzee reaches the height of three and a half to four feet. All the body, except the lower part,— the face, the palm, and back of the hand,— is covered with long, black hair. Herds of these animals are found in the large forests of Upper and Lower Guinea, and subsist on fruits and roots. They live on the ground by day, and by night in their nests, made of bent twigs, some twenty to thirty feet above the ground.

b. The Red ORANG-OUTANG (*Simia satyrus*) (*Pithecus satyrus*) is the Asiatic Orang, which, at present, inhabits only the marshy forests of Borneo, but not in large numbers. This ape was known to the Roman historian Pliny, since whose time it has often been brought into Europe, and has been studied in its minutest details by men like Cuvier, &c. Alas! this interesting animal, like the Chimpanzee, is carried off in a short time by consumption, in spite of the utmost care. Its extraordinary intelligence shows itself mostly during its sickness, when it willingly takes medicine, and every expression of its features reminds one of the suffering in a human being.

It is distinguished from the Chimpanzee, not only by the color, but by the length of the arms, which reach down to the ankles.

II. The GIBBONS, or LONGARMS (*Hylobates*), as their name signifies, are distinguished from all other apes, except the Orang, by the length of their arms.

They form a small group, of which only seven species are at present known. The Gibbon is a native of the East Indies.

c. The White-bearded GIBBON (*Simia lar*) (*Hylobates lar*) is one of the most agile of the family. It swings from one tree to another, a distance of thirty to forty feet, with the greatest ease, and can even change its direction while swinging, so that the swinging might rather be called flying.

d. The SIAMANG (*Simia Hylobates*) (*Hylobates syndac-*

tylus) is very large and heavy, three feet and a half in height; of a deep black color; a native of Sumatra. At the rising and setting of the sun, the Siamangs make a frightful noise, which can be heard at a great distance.

Plate 2.

a. The Brown Sapajou (*Cebus apella*). The Sapajou can be seen in almost any menagerie, and is preferable to most American monkeys. It is gentle and mild, and manifests great attachment to those who take care of it; it possesses a great degree of understanding, and knows how to make good use of its experience.

b. The Green, or St. Jago Monkey (*Cebus sabæus*). Only this monkey can easily be propagated in Europe. The back is of an olive-green color, belly white, and face black. They live upon the trees in the forests of Senegal.

c. The Dog-faced Baboon (*Cynocephalus*) has, as the name indicates (*cunos*, a dog; *cephale*, head), a face somewhat resembling a dog. Although very ferocious, Brehm found that the young female Baboons could be tamed, and showed great tractableness. Their manner of living, when free, is the same as other species of monkeys. They live in great herds in Asia and Africa, and subsist upon roots, leaves, fruits, and eggs. Full-grown animals attain the size of a large dog, and show surprising strength and boldness in fight.

d. The Mandril, or Ribbed-nosed Baboon (*Cynocephalus mormon*), is a native of the Gold-coast. They seek their food on rocks and trees. It is agreed that the Mandril is the ugliest of animals; not only in bodily, but in mental, characteristics. It has a short tail and long canine teeth; the nose and rump are scarlet-red, and the face is blue and wrinkled. It is very ferocious.

e. The COUXIO (*Stentor Beelzebub*) has a tufted beard. They live in troops in the forests of Brazil. It has received the name Stentor from the frightful, howling noise which it makes in the night, and which is heard at a great distance.

f. The BARBARY APE (*Inuus ecaudatus*) is now found only in Gibraltar, and in small numbers; formerly they were numerous in the mountains of North Africa, where they climbed the rocks to find worms, &c.; but they also knew how to take fruit from the trees.

PLATE 3.

a. The ARAGUATO (*Mycetes ursinus*) has the same properties as *e.* in Plate 2. The body is covered with a long, reddish hair; the beard is long, and the face is of a bluish-black color. The Araguatos are very common in Central South America: fifty have been counted on one tree. The frightful howling of the male can be heard at all hours of the day.

b. The Large-headed SAPAJOU (*Cebus capucinus*) is whitish around the face, the rest of the body is brown, but the shades of color are variable. It is very common.

c. The SIAMIRI (*Callithrix sciurea*). These are perhaps the most beautiful little monkeys in the New World. In their manner of living and motions, they resemble the squirrel more than the monkey. During the day, they are to be seen in large numbers on trees, particularly where the foliage is thick. They are too delicate to live any length of time in another climate.

d. The Silky TAMARIN (*Hapale rosalia*). This is one of the neatest and prettiest of animals, living in the woods of Brazil. It has a reddish-yellow mane, and the ends of the hair shine like gold in the open air It jumps from tree to tree like a squirrel, and, like it, lies down flat on a branch. The Tamarin cannot endure confinement.

e. The MAKI (*Lemur*) is a slim animal about the size of a common cat, with a foxlike head, fine woolly fur, and bushy tail. It hides in the holes of trees during the day, and comes out at sunset to roam through the woods. It lives upon trees, and subsists on fruits and the eggs of small birds. The Maki is found only in Madagascar.

PLATE 4.

a. The Flying DOG (*Pteropus edulis*) is a native of the East-India Islands, and the largest of the Bat family. Its hair is long and of a dark-brown color. Its head resembles that of a dog. It feeds on vegetables, and the natives of the Islands are obliged to cover their fruit-trees with nets to preserve the fruit from their devastations.

b. The VAMPIRE (*Vespertilio vampyrus*) (*Phyllostoma*) is found in Central South America; it hides during the day in clefts and caverns. At night, it hunts insects of all kinds, and does not reject the juicy fruits of the trees about whose tops it flutters. When pressed by hunger it attacks birds and mammals, sucking their blood through a hole which it pierces in their skin.

c. The Common BAT (*Vespertilio murinus*). This Bat is very generally diffused; it is found everywhere in Middle and Southern Europe and Asia, in the north of Africa; an allied species is found in North America. Just before sundown these bats are seen flying with the dexterity and steadiness of the swallow. Unfortunately, this useful little animal is very often sacrificed to superstition and unjust aversion. The ears of this bat are as large as its head; the tail is nearly as long as the body.

d. The Long-eared BAT (*Plecotus auritus*). This Bat, distinguished by the length of its ears, is very common in old houses in France. It flies late at night; and, though wanting the dexterity and steadiness of the common bat (*e.*), it is far superior in acuteness of hearing, as has been proved by experiments on one which was tamed.

e. The Horseshoe BAT (*Equinus vespertilio*) (*Rhinolophus*), so called from the form of a horseshoe on its nose. These bats are in Europe, what the Vampyre Bats are in Brazil; they have been observed sucking blood from birds, particularly hens and pigeons. They do not fly as easily as other bats, because the membranes which serve them for wings are shorter.

f. The Flying MAKI (*Galeopithecus volans*) is ten inches long and two feet wide. Like the Bats, this animal is active only during the night, when, aided by its sharp, hooked claws, it climbs to the tops of trees in search of fruits and insects. They are found in the Sunda and Moluccas Islands.

Plate 5.

a. The Civet (*Viverra zibetha*), a native of the East Indies, is two feet five inches long, without the tail, which is fifteen inches long. It is a beautiful, agile animal; but, like the Marten, extremely bloodthirsty. It sleeps the greater part of the day, but roams at night for prey, which consists of small mammals, birds, and their eggs. The odoriferous matter, called civet, is taken from the glands under the tail.

b. The Egyptian Rat, or Ichneumon (*Herpestes ichneumon*). A part of the thousand years' glory of this sacred animal of the ancient Egyptians has been preserved in the name Pharaoh's Rat, but *only* in this name. Its repute as a crocodile-killer and destroyer of crocodiles' eggs has been refuted by the observation of modern travellers; indeed, the Ichneumon is as much a hated animal with the Egyptians of the present day, as our Marten and Polecat are with us; for, like the latter, it commits its robberies in house and poultry-yard in open day; though it eats serpents, the chief food consists of mammals, and birds of all sorts.

c. The Mungos, or East-Indian Ichneumon (*Herpestes mungos*). The East-Indian Ichneumon, although much smaller, has the same boldness and inclination to rob as its larger cousin in Africa; but it is gentler and easier tamed; it is frequently used by the Japanese as a domestic animal for the destruction of rats and serpents; it is said to be extremely courageous in battle with poisonous serpents, and, when bitten, cures itself with Mungo-root, from which it derives its name.

d. The Common, or Pine MARTEN (*mustela martes*) lives in all parts of Europe and Central Asia. It builds its nest in the hollow trees of thick pine forests; it jumps, climbs, and swims extremely well; it is one of the most dexterous and boldest of robbers, against which no small animal is safe; the length is twenty inches; tail, twelve inches; the fine, soft hair is dark-brown on the top, and yellowish on the sides and lower part of the body.

e. The Stone MARTEN (*Mustela foina*) is chestnut-brown, with the under part of the throat and neck white; smaller and shorter than the common Marten; its manner of living is about the same, only that it approaches nearer human habitations, preferring to take up its abode in old walls, barns, &c.; it is fond of nice and sweet fruits; it is easily tamed when young; the gracefulness of its movements delights every lover of nature.

f. The POLECAT (*Mustela putorius*) (*Putorius communis*). This is the worst species in the whole family of Martens, and much disliked on account of the ravages it makes in the poultry-yard; it eats mice, rats, and serpents. The breast, feet, and tail of the Polecat are black. When attacked, it discharges a fluid of an insupportable odor, which effectually drives off the enemy.

PLATE 6.

a. The Common WEASEL (*Mustela vulgaris*) (*Putorius vulgaris*) is not larger than a common-sized rat; its small and lean body enables it not only to slip through cracks and holes in forest and field, but also in house and yard: so it happens that its usefulness in destroying mice, rats, and serpents is more than balanced by the devastation it makes among fowls and pigeons.

b. The ERMINE (*Putorius erminea*) (*Mustela erminea*) is almost twice as large as its little cousin; but otherwise much like it. In winter, and sometimes within a few days, the fur changes to a pure white, except on the tip of the tail, which remains always black. In its excursions for prey, which consists of all small animals in forest and field, as well as domestic fowl, it knows of no obstacle: it climbs nimbly, and swims rapidly, even over rough waters. The Ermine skins form, when sewed together, one of our finest and most valuable furs. Thousands of persons in North America and in Siberia are employed all winter in baiting traps for Ermines and Sables.

c. The FERRET (*Putorius furo*) (*Mustela furo*) has yellowish-white fur; it is a natural enemy of the Rabbit, on which account it is tamed, and made serviceable in hunting by driving the rabbits out from their burrows. The Ferret and Weasel kill their prey instantaneously.

d. The Sable MARTEN (*Mustela zibellina*) is brown, with gray spots upon the head. It is a native of Siberia, where it lives in burrows or hollow trees. Its fur is so valuable that hunters spend three or four winter months, enduring great hardship, in pursuit of it.

e. The SKUNK (*Mustela mephitis*) (*Mephitis mephitica*). This animal lives in America; is about the size of the Marten; it is furnished with long claws, with which it digs in the earth; it subsists on fruits, insects, and birds. Its long-haired fur is of a brilliant black, striped with white; the tail is long and bushy. The Skunk is feared by man and beast, on account of the fetid liquor which it ejects from glands situated near the anus. Five species are found in America.

f. The FISH OTTER (*Lutra vulgaris*) is found throughout Europe and the northern and central parts of Asia; its body is two feet eight inches long, and it attains the weight of from twenty to twenty-five pounds. It is a nocturnal animal, an excellent swimmer and diver. The Otter does not eat its prey in the water, but always brings it on land. The Fish Otter is often tamed when young, and proves a very intelligent animal; docile as a dog, it follows its master about, as affectionately as that fond animal.

"The American Otter is about four and a half feet long, including the tail, which is eighteen inches in length. The color is liver-brown above, slightly lighter beneath, sides of head and neck dirty-whitish. The fur is of two kinds: one, long, somewhat coarse, and scattered; the other, shorter, fine and dense."

g. The SEA OTTER (*Lutra marina*), twice as large as the Fish Otter, weighs from seventy to eighty pounds; it lives on the coast of the ocean between Asia and America, and is much hunted on account of its beautiful, black, shining, velvety fur. It subsists on crabs, mussels, and small fish.

PLATE 7.

The Cat Family (*Felinæ*). — Our common house-cat presents a good type of this whole family. Head round; eyes oblique, pupil rather oval, and capable of great expansion in darkness; whiskers long; canines sharp and very strong; body long; skin covered with soft hair, and everywhere loose; many animals of this family have a mane. The legs are of middling size and very strong; claws sheathed, and very sharp; tail long, and generally tufted on the end; step noiseless. They feed on mammals and birds, which they watch, especially in the night, and overpower with one spring; their senses, particularly those of sight and hearing, are well developed. They are possessed of moderate intellectual capacity. They are diffused over both the Old and New World, but do not pass beyond a certain northern limit, as cats are generally sensitive to cold.

a. The LION (*Felis leo*) is of a uniform tawny color; the body is from eight to nine feet long; tail three to four feet, and terminated by a tuft of hair. A beautiful mane ornaments the head, neck, and shoulders of the male. They inhabit Africa and the neighboring countries of Asia. There are several varieties of the Lion, that of Barbary (see plate) is considered the handsomest; that of Senegal is distinguished by the shortness of its mane. For perfect symmetry of the body, combined with the powerful development of the separate limbs, the Lion may justly be considered the king of beasts. His strength is extraordinary; he carries off an ox as easily as a cat carries a rat; with one stroke of his paw he can break the ribs of a horse, and with that of his tail throw the strongest man to the ground. His bearing is majestic; his roar resembles distant thunder, and fills all animals of the forest with terror; however, he is much less cruel than the tiger.

He feeds mostly on gazelles and monkeys. Although he fears man, and never attacks him except when pressed by hunger, he does not recoil at his presence, or that of any other animal. Lions live in pairs. The female is smaller than the male, and has no mane. Where there are European settlements their numbers have greatly diminished.

b. The TIGER (*Felis tigris*) is more slender, it is true, than the Lion, but in length it is equal, and in strength not inferior. It is a native of Asia, and a terrible animal; the number, in contradistinction to that of the Lion, does not diminish by the extension of European settlements, but seems rather to increase. Many people become prey to the rapacity of tigers; they live in continual warfare with each other, and often devour their own offspring.

c. The JAGUAR (*Felis onca*). This is the largest and strongest of the group of leopards, a representative of the tiger, to which he is scarcely inferior in size, in South America, where it is greatly feared as an animal of prey. Like the Lion, it is king of the forests where it lives; it chooses forests in the neighborhood of rivers for its abode, and hunts the tapir and other animals which go to the rivers to drink.

After having seen man for a few times, it loses the fear which it at first had of him, and boldly approaches his dwelling, carrying off dogs, horses, cattle, and even men themselves.

PLATE 8.

a. The LEOPARD (*Felis leopardus*) is a native of Africa and the warm countries of Asia. The color of its skin is more beautiful than that of any other animal of the cat family; it is a tawny-red color, with black spots somewhat in the form of rosettes. Every motion of its elegant body is agile and graceful. Bold, like the Lion, it surpasses this proud, generous robber in catlike slyness. It is exceedingly bloodthirsty, and makes fearful ravages among flocks and herds.

A full-grown male measures six and a half feet, including the tail; and is about two and a half feet in height.

b. The PUMA, or American LION (*Felis concolor*), has been called the Silver Lion on account of the silver-gray color of the lower body and legs. It is a slender animal, with small, gray head, strong paws, and thin tuftless tail; the skin of the back is a smooth, dark, yellowish-red; mane wanting. Called Panther and Catamount in North America. The Puma is much weaker than the Jaguar, and cannot, like this, seize upon large animals, but must content itself with those of the size of a sheep, of which it has been known to carry off fifty in a single night. On that account, every effort is made to exterminate it. It is hunted with dogs, which chase it up the trees, where it is shot.

c. The LYNX (*Felis lynx*) has a reddish-brown skin, with spots of a deeper shade; pointed ears and short tail. It is three and a half feet long, and the largest kind of cat which still exists in a wild state. The Lynx is a very voracious animal, and commits great depredations among flocks and game. Mornings and evenings it pounces upon stags, sheep, and goats, not disdaining the smaller mammals and birds. It conceals itself in the foliage of high trees to watch for prey; when it judges that the animal cannot escape, it springs upon and destroys it. If obliged to make many springs, it gives up the chase. The skin is valuable for fur.

d. The Wild CAT (*Felis catus fera*). A brindled, fierce animal, which frequents retired woods and copses among rocks; its tail is of uniform thickness, with black rings; body, about two and a half feet long; tail, one foot. The Wild Cat climbs the highest trees with the greatest facility; hunts birds, rabbits, &c., and even fish; catches a great number of mice and moles. It is a dangerous animal, and, if slightly wounded, turns upon the hunter with great ferocity.

e. The Domestic CAT (*Felis domestica*) is too generally known to need to be described. According to modern investigation, it seems to have descended from the Nubian Cat; and from Egypt, by degrees, it has been spread over all the world. The House Cat is amiable and very intelligent; she is much attached to man, but more to the house. That she is false is a simple calumny, and an aversion to cats is unjustifiable and absurd.

PLATE 9.

DOGS (*Canes*). In this family are comprised the real dogs, wolves, foxes, and hyenas. Dogs in general have a small head with pointed muzzle, thin legs, and small paws; the fore paws have five, the back four toes, with unsheathed claws; the tail is proportionally short and bushy. All their senses are exceedingly well developed, especially smell and hearing: they are not shaped for climbing; but, instead, they are expert in running, digging, and swimming. Those in the service of man are noted for their intellectual capacities. They are not like cats, strictly carnivorous, but some of them live on vegetables, and tame dogs eat every thing. The whole earth is their home; even Australia, poor in animals, has its wild dog, or dingo.

Whilst the bloodthirsty propensities of the Cat are often concealed by the beauty of her form and the softness of her fur, the gloomy appearance of the Hyena always gives a bad impression. Its strong head, oblique eyes, thick neck, short-set, rugged body, with bristly mane and sloping back, altogether make it a very homely animal. The voice of the Hyena sometimes resembles the whining of a child and sometimes a disagreeable laugh, which has given rise to the various stories related by nurses of those countries which they inhabit. Their greediness, extending over both living and dead animals, is as well known as their cowardice. They live in Asia and Africa. Mussulmen consider them unclean and detestable animals.

a. The Striped HYENA (*Hyæna striata*), the most common, is distributed over the hottest parts of Asia and Africa. The length of the body is five feet; color yellowish-gray, with brown and black stripes; the large upright ears are bare. This Hyena is seen in all menageries; among other abominations related of it, is that of digging up bodies in burial-grounds. It lives principally on carcasses of animals and all kinds of refuse, for which it roams about in the night.

b. The Spotted HYENA (*Hyæna picta*). This is much larger and stronger than the Striped Hyena, and, although cowardly by nature, if tortured by hunger, does not hesitate to attack middling-sized animals, and even man; but the latter only when in sleep. The native land of the Spotted Hyena is South and East Africa.

The real dog has so much in common with the wolf, that a general description will answer for both: however, it may be difficult for some to consider the terrier or badger dog as near relations to the wolf; but size and form do not decide the question. The skull, the teeth, and manner of living, designate the family to which an animal belongs. Dogs and wolves have a long skull with a projecting muzzle: the pupil of the eye is round; the body lean, and narrowed toward the hips; legs slim and sinewy; senses well developed, particularly that of smell, which guides the animal in finding its food. The whole family manifests an inclination for society, which unites the wild kinds into great herds. The dog hunts by day.

No animal is so completely identified with the existence of man as the dog; none has so faithfully followed him everywhere.

Whence come so many forms of the House Dog (*Canis domesticus*) is not positively known; though it is supposed to be through natural and artificial breeding and crossing of different kinds of wolves. All house dogs, however different in size, form, and character, are alike in their attachment to man, and capacity to adapt themselves to his customs. Intellectually, they are highly gifted animals, possessing good memory, great understanding, and much feeling. They stand high also in physical characters. Their quickness combines with their endurance, their strength with their agility, in making them almost indispensable to man. The Poodle is considered, by Scheitlin, as the most perfect of dogs.

c. The GREYHOUND (*Canis grajus*) is only valuable for hunting in extensive grass-covered plains; notwithstanding, it is kept chiefly in Hungary, the southern part of Russia, and by all nomad tribes in Asia and Africa, for chasing hares, antelopes, &c. It is easily recognized by the long, pointed head, thin body, full arched chest, and long legs. Its sight and hearing are acute, but the sense of smell is less fine than that of other hunting dogs. It is accused of falseness in character.

d. The Hunting Dog (*Canis venaticus*) is of middling size and strong build; ears long, broad, and hanging. It displays wonderful consideration and skill when hunting for feathered game.

e. The WOLF (*Canis lupus*) is different from the Dog in form, character, and manner of living. The wild dog bears the nearest resemblance to the Wolf, which might be taken for a long-haired wild dog, only that it lets its tail hang, while the former carries it up, and often with an inclination to the left. The length of the Wolf, including the tail, is five feet; height, two feet; the color is a mixture of yellow, gray, and brownish-red. It is devoid of the noble courage of the Dog, and with all its strength is a cowardly animal, risking life only when driven by extreme hunger; the voice is a disagreeable howl. It is considered the natural enemy of man, who uses all means to exterminate it wherever found.

Plate 10.

a. The JACKAL (*Canis aureus*) resembles the Wolf, but is smaller; the tail is short and bushy; color, yellowish-brown; it is two feet long and one and a half high, and lives in herds in the warmest parts of Asia and Africa; it is also found in Dalmatia. Its habits are similar to those of a Hyena; the food, likewise, consists of carcasses and wild and tame mammals.

Foxes are distinguished from domestic dogs and wolves by the form of their skull, long sharp nose, oval pupil, and bushy tail, sometimes called brush.

b. The Fox (*Canis vulpes*) needs no particular description; its slyness and cunning calculation, its boldness and impudence, have been well known from the earliest times. It lives on poultry, hares, &c., and when pressed by hunger takes mice, lizards, insects, and vegetable substances. It makes holes in the earth, or takes possession of those of other animals.

Having spoken of those animals which subsist on warm-blooded animals, we now turn to those which feed on insects; thus nature fills all space. What escapes the bats in the air, falls as prey to those animals which hunt on the earth and in the water for insects. Such are the smallest mammals: thick-set, strong-bodied; snouts trunk-like and long; teeth perfect, sharp and cutting; limbs short; tail moderate. In these animals some of the senses are obtuse, while others are acute. They are very shy, and hide in holes and clefts of rocks: some live in the water, and others on trees; in cold climates they sleep during the winter, in warm ones they are continually active; under all circumstances, they are very useful in destroying multitudes of insects and snails.

c. The HEDGEHOG (*Erinaceus Europæus*). A very harmless creature, found about hedges, and called Hedgehog from its head and snout being somewhat like those of a hog. Its back is covered with prickles. It moves very slowly, and, when danger threatens, rolls itself into a ball, and presents a somewhat formidable appearance. It creeps about at night in quest of insects, small mammals, and birds; also fruits and roots.

d. The Common SHREW (*Sorex araneus*), though much feared by many people, is a harmless little creature, only ten inches in length and five in height (the female is a little longer). It has a small head, with truncated snout, broad short ears, and small eyes. Cats kill this animal, but refuse to eat it, on account of its disagreeable odor.

e. The Water SHREW (*Sorex fodiens*) is a little larger than the preceding: black above and white below; it lives near the borders of rivers, and swims with great facility.

f. The Pigmy SHREW (*Sorex pigmæus*) is of a grayish-brown color above, and white below. This is the smallest of the class of Mammalia; it is found chiefly around the coast of the Adriatic Sea.

g. The Common MOLE (*Talpa*) digs subterranean galleries for its dwelling, and buries itself deeper and deeper in winter, but is never in a torpid state. It is furnished with strong spade-like fore legs, well adapted by their size and position for digging in the ground. The mole lives upon worms and insects, particularly the larvæ of Beetles (improperly called white-worms), by which it renders great service to man. The eyes are extremely small, and concealed by the thick fur on the head; external ears wanting; however, it has a very large tympanum, and fine sense of hearing. The fur of the mole is soft, and was formerly used in the manufacture of hats.

Plate 11.

The BEAR (*Ursus*) is a large animal with stout limbs, short ears, small eyes, and short tail; the hair is very thick, which makes it look larger than it really is. In walking, it puts the flat soles of the feet upon the earth; the strong paws have five toes with very sharp claws; the teeth seem made rather for vegetable than animal food. The senses of smell and hearing predominate. What the larger kind of bears lack in agility is made up in strength and endurance. The Bear is still found in the uncivilized countries of Europe, Asia, and America.

a. The Black BEAR (*Ursus Americanus*) inhabits the thick forests of North America, where it lives mostly on vegetable substances, although it is said to attack herds of cattle, and tear the strongest of them to pieces. Generally, it is a quiet, harmless animal, which, in spite of its enormous size, is less to be feared than the European Bear, somewhat smaller. It is distinguished by its lustrous black coat, and the yellowish color of its muzzle.

b. The Brown BEAR (*Ursus arctos*) is rather smaller than the Black Bear. It is found in the mountainous countries of Europe and Asia, and attains the height of six feet. It walks slowly, and leads a solitary life in the thick forests; its brown fur changes color with age and climate. When young, it lives chiefly on vegetable food; with age, it becomes ferocious; ruler of the district in which it lives, it is feared by all animals. The somewhat dangerous hunting for this Bear begins when it is fat, and prepared to retire for its winter's sleep; it pays well, as the meat is a delicacy, and the fur valuable.

c. The Ice, or Polar, BEAR (*Ursus maritimus*) has a smooth, white fur and long head. One was shot which measured eight feet, and weighed one thousand six hundred pounds.

The Ice Bear belongs to the northern hemispheres, and inhabits exclusively the icy coasts of the polar seas; it is sometimes carried to Norway and Iceland by blocks of ice. As awkward as it looks, it runs swiftly, and has no superior in swimming; it is a bold animal, confiding in its own strength and fearing no danger; it lives on fish, seals, walruses, and whatever the sea and coast offer.

d. The RACCOON (*Procyon lotor*), contrary to its giant-like relatives, is a neat animal two feet long, without the ten-inch tail, and one foot high. Generally, it remains lying in hollow trees during the day, and comes out at twilight in search of fruits, insects, and worms. It has the peculiar habit of washing its food when not pressed by hunger.

PLATE 12.

a. The GLUTTON (*Gulo borealis*) has, in form and manner of living, much resemblance to the bears, with which it was formerly classed; but the Glutton is in reality a great heavy Marten, with thick-set body, arched on the back, short neck and short strong legs; the five-toed paws are armed with sharp claws; the tail is short and bushy; it is from two and a half to three feet long and one and a half feet high. The Glutton, in spite of its ominous name, eats no more or less than it needs. In its inhospitable home, which extends over the north part of the earth, it lives on whatever it can get, — marmots, white grouse, &c.; also reindeer and elks, on whose back it jumps from the trees. It is not agile in its motions, but enduring; the skin is valuable as fur.

b. The BADGER (*Meles vulgaris*) is brown above and black below; head white, with a black line on each side. The tail is short; and the long hair covers its legs, so that the body seems very near the earth. The Badger makes two entrances to its burrow, which it furnishes with straw, dried leaves, and moss, and keeps extremely neat. It feeds on roots, fruits, insects, and mice; and leads a solitary life in its artistic, comfortable structure under the earth, where it sleeps away the whole winter with slight interruptions. It seeks its food in the night.

MARSUPIALS. — The Marsupials are all confined to Australia, with the adjacent islands, and America.

c. The OPOSSUM (*Didelphis*) reaches the size of a domestic cat; has a short, thick neck, and clumsy, heavy body. This animal has received the name of Pedimane on account of the peculiar construction of its hind feet, which somewhat resemble a hand. The female has a pouch or pocket (formed by a fold of the abdomen), where she puts her little ones, which have scarcely a distinct form at their birth. Here they remain until fully developed, when they leave the pouch, into which they return if danger threatens. The Opossum is a nocturnal animal; it feeds on birds, and sometimes finds its way into poultry-yards and kills the fowl. It is very dextrous in climbing, and frequently holds itself suspended by its prehensile tail to watch its prey. The Opossum is a native of America.

d. The KANGAROO (*Macropus*) is one of the largest of the family, also the largest animal of Australia. An old male in a sitting posture is as tall as a man; its body is eight feet, tail two feet and a half long. It is much hunted by the natives and by the English with Kangaroo dogs, for its beautiful fur and savory meat; on that account it retires farther and farther from the coast of New South Wales, where it was first discovered. It becomes easily accustomed to European vegetable food, and, when well cared for, will live fifteen years in confinement.

Gnawing animals, RODENTIA. It is only necessary to look into the mouth of these animals to recognize them immediately. In each jaw they have two chisel-shaped incisors, between which and the molars there is a wide space without teeth. The neck is short and thick, eyes large and prominent; the organs of sense are well developed, but their intellectual capacities are small. In regard to food, they play a great part in the economy of nature, by eating of all kinds of vegetable substances; moreover, they are spread over all the earth, and multiply astonishingly.

Porcupines are great gnawers; they are distinguished by their thick-set body, quilled skin, and grunting voice. They inhabit the temperate and warm climates of the

Old and New World. Some are short tailed, and live on the earth, during the daytime, however, in holes; others have a long tail, and climb trees. They feed on fruits and roots.

e. The PORCUPINE (*Hystrix cristatus*) is two feet long and about nine inches high. It has a long mane of stiff bristles. Its quills, mixed with bristles, are set loose in the skin, so that many fall out when the animal shakes its skin; this circumstance has given rise to the saying that the animal throws his quills against an enemy. The Porcupine is found in the north of Africa, the south of Italy, and in Greece. Its food consists of roots, which it seeks only at night. It is easily kept in confinement; but is a stupid, lazy animal.

f. The GUINEA PIG (*Cavia*) was taken from South America to Europe, where it has become domesticated; it is no longer to be found wild in its original home. The form and color of this animal, as well as its wonderful fecundity, are generally known. It is neither a pig, nor does it come from Guinea.

PLATE 13.

a. The AGOUTI (*Dasyprocta aguti*) resembles the Hare, from which it can be distinguished by its short ears and the form of its feet; the front ones are short, and have four toes, hinder ones twice as long, with three toes. The shining, rough hair is reddish-yellow, mixed with dark brown.

The Agouti lives in the northern part of South America. It is quick in its movements, cautious, and shy. Its food is roots, leaves, and grain. It is easily bred in Europe.

b. The HAMSTER (*Cricetus vulgaris*) resembles a considerably plump mouse, with cheek-pouches, a thick body of a foot long, and a short, hairy tail. It is reddish-brown above, and black below, with white feet. However, these colors are changeable.

The Hamster is one of the most injurious of animals, carrying off large quantities of grain into its hole, which is sometimes seven feet deep. This unsocial creature is a perfect miser, not allowing even its mate to enter its storehouse. The Hamster is very common in sandy plains, from the north of Germany to Siberia. Great pains are taken to extirpate Hamsters, and their numbers would be much more considerable if they did not wage continual war upon each other.

c. The MARMOT, or Mountain RAT (*Arctomys marmotta*), inhabits the Alps, Pyrenees, and Carpathian Mountains, and even the highest points immediately below the region of perpetual snow, where it sleeps away more than two-thirds of the year in its well-protected winter-quarters. In summer, it descends farther down the mountains, and feeds on roots and grass. Notwithstanding its foresight, it is persecuted by man, who shoots it in summer, and digs it out of its hole in winter. The flesh is savory, and the fur soft and warm. The American Marmot is called Woodchuck and Ground Hog.

Squirrels of various kinds are found all over the earth, with the exception of New Holland, and are the prettiest and liveliest of the Rodents. The Squirrel has a delicate head and large eyes; rather long, hairy tail; the hind legs longer than the fore legs. They live in holes in the earth, and chase each other from tree to tree. Those of the colder climates wander south, or sleep through the winter.

d. The SQUIRREL (*Sciurus vulgaris*) is an ornament to forest-trees wherever found. Their tufted ears and the bushy tail, which they throw over the back while sitting on their hind legs, give them a peculiarly handsome appearance. Agile as monkeys, they spring from tree to tree, using their tail as a sort of rudder; their color, differing according to country and season, is of every shade, from a reddish-brown to black. They sleep away the nights, rainy days, and nearly the whole winter; for the latter, they provide themselves with a store of nuts, &c. Their nests are similar to those of the Magpie and Jay; sometimes they sleep in hollow trees. Their chief enemy is the Marten.

The DORMICE (*Myoxus*). These have great similarity, in the structure of their bodies, to Squirrels; but differ in the manner of living; in the number of vertebræ and ribs; beside, they have a more pointed and mouselike head, and a double rowed, bushy tail. Unlike the Squirrels, which are lively in the daytime, they lead a nocturnal life in search of fruits and seeds, and hide themselves in holes and crevices of the rocks during the day; they also sleep in the winter. They are found in the temperate zones.

e. The DORMOUSE (*Myoxus glis*) is chiefly at home in the south and east of Europe, where it chooses the dry oak and beech forests. It measures eleven inches from nose to tail, which is five inches long. Dormice are pretty little animals, with soft fur and hairy and tufted tail; color, ash-gray above, shaded down to white. The old Romans kept them by hundreds, to be fattened for the tables of the rich; even now they are hunted, partly for their flesh, partly for their fur.

The real Mice are the most numerous family of the small Rodentia, and have become more injurious than most other gnawers on account of their great numbers. The Mice have a pointed head, with large eyes and broad ears. Their body is generally slender, and they have fine, smooth hairy coats; the tail is long or short, hairy or naked; feet, delicate, five-toed and sharp-clawed. Mice inhabit all the countries of the earth; they can exist wherever vegetables are to be found. They follow man everywhere, and are sly gnawers, gifted with sharp senses. They are persecuted because they destroy so much food.

f. The Field Mouse (*Mus arvalis*) is one of the most injurious of the Rodentia; it is five and a half inches long, of a yellowish-gray color above, and dirty white below; it lives in the fields, where it builds passage-ways and chambers under the ground to store up grain, nuts, &c., for the winter; it comes into human habitations to eat of the food kept in cellars. The Field Mice increase enormously in dry seasons; driven by hunger, they emigrate in large numbers, and even swim across rivers.

g. The Domestic Mouse (*Mus musculus*) was, even in the oldest times, a *too* much attached companion of man; at present, there is scarcely a spot on earth inhabited by him where it is not to be found. In spite of its nibbling and gnawing, no one, who observes its graceful movements and cleanly habits, can really hate it. The fecundity of the Mouse is enormous: a single pair multiplies to thirty in one year; for which reason man is obliged to put a stop to such increase, — a task in which he is aided by the cat, weasel, marten, eagle, owl, &c. The Mouse is an intelligent, sly, little animal, with acute senses, among which hearing is the most prominent.

h. The Black RAT (*Mus rattus*), one of our most noxious vermin, is said to have originated in the East. It is a famous burrower, eating its way through almost any substance. Rats are very destructive, and are difficult to destroy, when once they have made an entrance into a house.

The Brown, or Norway, RAT (*Mus decumanus*), a little larger than the former, follows man everywhere; indeed, rats are at home in all human habitations; they live in society, but often make war upon and kill each other.

i. The Wood MOUSE (*Mus sylvaticus*) is a little larger than the Domestic Mouse. It is of a grayish-brown color above, and white below. Although it does much injury in fields and woods, it is not confined to them, but makes its way into houses, where it eats of all that kitchen and cellar offer. Wood Mice often emigrate from one country to another, and are said to march in straight lines.

k. The Blind MOUSE (*Spalax typhlus*) is distinguished by its large head; broad paws, with strong claws; absence of tail, and, more than all, by the smallness of its eyes, which are covered by skin. It is found chiefly in Hungary, Russia, and Western Asia.

HARES (*Lepores*) are spread over all the earth, with the exception of New Holland, and are too well known to need description.

a. The Common HARE (*Lepus timidus*) is about two and a quarter feet long, with a short up-turned tail. It has large, timid eyes, very long ears, and long hind legs. It is colored very much of the same hue as that of the brownish-gray places where it conceals itself. Its flesh is savory, and its skin much used by hatters. During the winter, it lives in the woods; during summer and autumn, in the fields. Notwithstanding the Hare is hunted, not only by man, but by foxes and birds of prey, it increases rapidly. It is common in Central Europe, and the western part of Asia.

b. The White, or Changing, HARE (*Lepus variabilis*) is somewhat smaller than the Field Hare, its head is rounder, ears shorter, hind legs longer, and the soles of its feet more hairy. This Hare turns white to the black tips of the ears, as soon as the first snow falls; in spring, it becomes gray again.

Like all Alpine animals, it is timid and shy. It inhabits the high mountains of the south of Europe.

c. The RABBIT (*Lepus cuniculus*) is every way smaller than the Hare: in a wild state, it is of a reddish-gray; when tame, its color is variable. It appears to have originated in Spain, but is spread throughout Europe and North America. Rabbits multiply prodigiously; they are great burrowers, and hence their Latin name of Cuniculus, from which comes their popular name of Coney.

The Beaver forms a family in itself.

d. The BEAVER (*Castor fiber*) has a wide scale-covered tail and webbed feet. This creature is quite at home in the water. It is found in lonely, damp places, near lakes and rivers, in the north of Europe and in North America. Its fine fur and size make it a valuable fur-producing animal. It has under its tail two large glandulous pouches, containing a viscid secretion of strong and penetrating odor, much employed in medicine under the name of Castor. The Beaver constructs huts for its winter residence, and forms dams across streams of water.

e. The MUSKRAT (*Fiber zibethicus*) has a long tail, fur of a reddish-gray color. It is about a foot in length, and resembles a Rat. Like the Beaver, it has two glands under its tail, which secrete a fluid having a strong odor of musk. It lives on the borders of rivers and lakes in North America; and, like the Beaver, it constructs huts in which to pass the winter.

PLATE 15.

a. EDENTATA. The ANT-EATER (*Myrmecophaga*), has a long muzzle, terminated by a small circular mouth, a handsome mane running along its back, and a long, tufted tail. It has no teeth. Its tongue is from three to four inches in length, and can be stretched half a foot out of its mouth. This singular animal feeds on ants and termites, introducing its long, sticky tongue into their nests; when it is covered with ants, it draws it out quickly, and swallows all the insects at once. Ant-eaters are mostly found in Paraguay, where they prove to be very useful animals in destroying the nests of ants and termites, with their long, sharp claws.

b. The DUCK-BILLED QUADRUPED (*Ornithorhynchus paradoxus*) attains the length of twenty inches, including the tail, which is broad and flat. It has a beaver-like body, with thick, reddish-brown fur. It has but four teeth, and those are without roots, and in the back part of the mouth. The external ear is also wanting. This curious animal lives in New Holland, on the borders of marshes and rivers. It constructs subterranean galleries from twenty to fifty feet long, from which it goes out into the mud in search of insects.

c. The Scaly PANGOLIN (*Manis*). The head of this animal is short and thick; trunk, broad; tail, almost as long as the body. The Pangolin is covered with scales, and has long and very strong nails; when full grown, it measures about four feet. It is a native of Central Africa.

d. The ARMADILLO (*Dasypus*) has upon its back six, and sometimes seven, movable rows of plates, forming a sort of cuirass; the part of the body which is free from the plates is covered with a warty, wrinkled skin. Behind the neck, and between the rows of plates, are stiff bristles. This animal inhabits Central and South America. It digs holes in the earth, and eats worms, insects, fruits, and leaves. Its flesh is edible.

e. The SLOTH (*Bradypus*) has claws so strong, that when clinging to the branch of a tree it is almost impossible to bring it away. Its fur is ash-gray, or grayish-brown; on either side of the back are broad brown stripes running down to the tail. It sleeps suspended to the branch of a tree. It is found in the great forests of Brazil.

Plate 16.

a. The RHINOCEROS (*Rhinoceros indicus*): a characteristic specimen of the Pachydermata, or thick-skinned quadrupeds, and so named from the Greek words, signifying *nose* and *horn*. That figured on the plate is the Indian Rhinoceros; it is easily recognized by the single horn, and by the plaited skin. The African species have two horns and smooth skins.

This animal can force its way through the thickest and most thorny brushwood; and, when roused to anger, is a formidable assailant. It lives on vegetable substances, which it can hook up with the prolongation of its upper lip, acting somewhat like a small proboscis. Intellectually, it is far beneath the Elephant; the clumsy creature lies for hours in a pond, or moves sluggishly forward; but is easily excited, when, in blind fury, it tramples down all that comes in its way.

b. The ELEPHANT (*Elephas*) is the largest of terrestrial animals; its ordinary height is from ten to fourteen feet. It inhabits the warmest countries of Asia and Africa, and lives on vegetables. There are two species of elephants: the Indian Elephant, which is domesticated, and is used as a beast of burden; and the African, which cannot be tamed, but is hunted for ivory. The Elephant lives in troops; feeds on leaves and branches, which it breaks off with the trunk; and is, if not irritated, a harmless, peaceable creature. In the service of man, as a domestic animal, for which it has been used since the earliest times, it displays a wonderful intelligence and reflection, equalled only by the dog.

By means of the trunk, it can root up a pine, throw down a tiger, and take up the smallest object. It is said that one of these animals, in a domestic state, eats daily one hundred pounds of rice, and as much hay.

Plate 17.

a. The Tapir (*Tapirus suillus*) (*T. Americanus*). This animal is found in South America. The female, which is about six feet long, is larger and stronger than the male. Its dark-brown color is somewhat lighter on the breast and neck. Its mane is short and stiff. The Tapir is a harmless, peaceful animal, furnished with a trunk-like upper lip; its manner of living is said to resemble that of the Hog. It subsists principally on fruits and herbs.

b. The Hippopotamus, or River Horse (*Hippopotamus amphibius*), is from ten to twelve feet long, and weighs some two thousand pounds; its legs are not more than two feet long; skin, bluish-brown and hairless; head and snout, large; eyes and ears, small. The Hippopotamus lives on the borders of rivers in the central and southern parts of Africa. It remains in the reeds or in the water during the day, and swims and plunges with great facility. At night, it overruns the country, making great havoc in the millet and rice plantations. It is naturally peaceable; but, when provoked, attacks its enemy with great fury. The skin is so thick that a musket-ball cannot penetrate it. The flesh is good to eat; the canine teeth furnish the most beautiful ivory, and the skin makes good leather.

c. The Domestic Hog (*Sus domesticus*). It would be superfluous to give a description of an animal, everywhere so generally known as the Hog.

d. The Wild Hog, or Boar (*Sus ferus*), is found in Europe, Asia, and the north of Africa. It is a very strong animal, and, in comparison with the Domestic Hog, is very agile. Its head is longer and more pointed; tusks, particularly in the male, are longer and sharper; color, a very dark brown. The Wild Hog lives, in larger or smaller herds, in thick woods away from the habitations of men; but, when it goes out at night, it does much injury in the fields, trampling down and rooting up more than it eats. The flesh, skin, and bristles are all used.

Plate 18.

Ruminantia. — This order comprises all those animals which masticate their food the second time, or which chew the cud.

a. The Dromedary (*Dromedarius*) has but one hump; its hair is fine and flaxy, gray or brown; its body is about five feet long. This animal is found in the north of Africa, in Arabia and Persia, everywhere in a domesticated state. It has been acclimated in Tuscany for two hundred years.

b. The Camel (*Camelus bactrianus*) has two humps on its back. It is larger and stronger than the Dromedary. It is employed in Northern and Central Asia, its native land, as a beast of burden. The Camel is not found in Arabia or Africa. It is highly prized by the nomad tribes, to whom it is almost indispensable in crossing the sandy deserts; besides, its flesh is savory, milk good, and wool used for clothing.

Plate 19.

a. The Lama (*Auchenia lama*), when wild, is about the size of a Stag; its hair is long and brown, but changes color when domesticated. It is found on the mountains of Peru in herds of two or three hundred. The Lama is much esteemed on account of its flesh, but more as a beast of burden, in which respect it is unsurpassed. It can travel six or eight leagues a day over steep mountain paths, with a hundred pounds upon its back, and is satisfied with the herbs it finds on its way.

b. The Musk Deer (*Moschus moschiferus*) is an elegant animal, the size of a Roe. It has a fine head without antlers, short neck, and slender legs. Its fur is reddish-brown, with long hair on the side. The male is distinguished by its long canine teeth, which grow two or three inches beyond its mouth; and by a pouch under its belly, which contains from an ounce to an ounce and a half of the well-known article called musk. This extremely timid and agile animal lives in the mountains of China, Thibet, and the central and southern parts of Siberia.

c. The Elk (*Cervus alces*). A peculiar and imposing-looking animal, which does not seem to belong to the present creation. It is from eight to eight and a half feet long, and six feet high; a giant among the Deer. The Elk has a thick, long muzzle; small, dull eyes, and long ass-like ears; neck, strong and powerful;

body heavy, with feet proportionately large and strong. The full-grown male has powerful broadly palmated horns, thick and strong mane; the color of the hair is brown. It runs rapidly, and if wounded defends itself with hoofs and antlers. The American Elk is called Moose.

PLATE 20.

a. The REINDEER (*Cervus tarandus*) is smaller and fleeter than the Elk; its hoofs are broad and almost cow-like. Both sexes have antlers, those of the female being rather smaller than those of the male; their large antlers are bent, and divided into many branches. The Reindeer is brown in summer, and almost white in winter. There is a great difference between those that live free in the mountains and those domesticated by man: the latter are kept in large herds, and are, perhaps, the most useful of animals. They are used for draught and burden; their milk is very nourishing; their flesh, excellent; their skin furnishes good fur and strong leather; spoons and other utensils are made from their bones; and their tendons and sinews are used for ropes and thread. These animals are generally very gentle; they subsist on leaves, moss, and lichens. They are found in the northern parts of the Old and New World.

b. and *c.* The STAG (*Cervus elaphus*) is the most stately and handsomest of the European Deer; seven feet in length, and four and a half feet in height. It has a slender body, elegant legs, and fine large antlers on a well-formed head. The old Stag sheds the antlers at the end of February; the young ones, in March or May:

five or six days after the new antlers come out, and are fully developed in from ten to twelve weeks. At first they are covered with a velvety skin, which, when dried, the Stag rubs off against the trees. This animal is spread over all Europe and a part of Asia. It feeds on herbs, leaves, fruits, &c.

Plate 21.

a. The Common Fallow Deer (*Cervus dama*) is smaller than the Stag; a gentle and timid creature. The horns of the male are broad, and fingered at the end, and there are two snags, or spurred branches, springing from each in front. The color of the coat, in summer, is reddish-brown with white spots; in winter it is dark-gray, but changes with the age of the animal. This Deer is common in Europe, but is supposed to have originated in Barbary.

b. and *c.* The Roe (*Cervus capreolus*) is an elegant little creature, and very fleet. Although occasionally caught when young, and tamed, the Roe is never perfectly subdued, always retaining more or less of its original wildness. They keep close to the shelter of woods and copses, and seldom venture, like other deer, into plains. Thirst alone induces them to leave their native woods, and go to some running stream. Hunting this Deer is very profitable; for, besides its flesh bringing a good price, its skin and horns are much used.

d. The Klip Springer (*Antilope oreotragus*). The male is ornamented with short, straight, black horns, which stand perpendicularly on the head; it has no beard, and the tail is short. The Klip Springers are nimble and beautiful animals, found in the mountains of the Cape and Abyssinia, where they live like the Chamois, which they resemble, on odorous herbs; and, like it, spring from one cleft to another; they live in herds, and are hunted for their flesh and their skin.

Plate 22.

a. The GIRAFFE (*Camelopardalis*) has short horns, covered by a velvety skin, and extremely long neck; its back is inclined, body short, skin whitish, spotted with yellow; its fore legs are much longer than its hind ones; eyes beautiful, and eyelids of a dark color. It is the tallest of all the mammiferous animals, and can reach eighteen feet high. The Giraffe is very gentle, and feeds on leaves and grass; its gait, in walking, is very awkward. It is a native of Central and Southern Africa; it is not easily acclimated, and therefore seldom seen in zoölogical gardens and menageries.

b. The CHAMOIS (*Antilope rupicapra*) is distinguished by its straight horns, which are suddenly bent back, like hoops, at the ends; it has great resemblance to the Goat, only that its body is stouter and legs longer. Its length is three feet, ten inches; height, two feet, four inches. Both sexes are perfectly alike in color and form; but the male becomes stouter, and has larger horns. As with other mountain animals, for example the Alpine Hare, the color of the Chamois changes according to the season, and is wonderfully adapted to its surroundings; therefore the general color in summer is a dingy reddish-brown, somewhat lighter under the body; in winter, on the contrary, it is dark-brown above, and white below. The Chamois needs this protection from nature; for in spite of their acute senses, carefulness, and precaution, astonishing agility in springing and climbing, their numbers have greatly diminished by the persecution of animals and men. Formerly there were herds of forty, now there are seldom more than twenty, seen together. Such herds are assembled only in autumn, at other seasons the sexes live apart. The Chamois are found upon the Alps, the mountains of Greece, Dalmatia, the Carpathians, and the mountains in the south of France.

c. The GAZELLE (*Antilope dorcas*). This beautiful inhabitant of the desert and steppes of North Africa has always been considered by the Arabs (who are so much in sympathy with nature, and susceptible to its beauties) as the perfect picture of beauty; and, indeed, if we may judge by the reports of travellers, there cannot be a more attractive, agreeable, and impressive sight than a group of these lovely animals pasturing under the shadow of a mimosa. The eyes of the Gazelle are large and expressive, and its noble head is ornamented with spiral horns in the form of a lyre. Its neck is long and slender; its nicely rounded body rests upon fine, sinewy legs, with elegant little hoofs. The reddish-yellow color of its back is separated from the white underneath by a brownish-black line, as seen in the picture. This animal, though beautiful when at rest, is still more so when leaping light and nimbly over the desert. The Arabs hunt this animal, for which their horses are scarcely a match in fleetness, with greyhounds and falcons; also with the hunting leopard.

Plate 23.

a. The Bull (*Bos taurus*), (*b.*) The Cow (*Bos taurus f.*) are found everywhere, and their utility is generally known. The varieties of the common ox are numerous.

c. The Musk Ox (*Bos moschatus*) (*Ovibos moschatus*) is the smallest of this family, and bears more resemblance to a sheep than an ox; its legs are short, and its body is covered with thick, long, brown hair; its horns, which are bent downward and then upward, are two feet long, and an extremely dangerous weapon. It lives in the northern part of North America and Greenland; feeds on grass in summer; and in winter, on moss and lichens. It can climb rocks with the facility of a goat. Its flesh has a strong odor of musk, and is not good for food.

d. Zebu (*Bos zebu*). This holy ox of the Hindoos is strikingly marked by the large hump over its shoulders, and its short, flat horns. The Zebu is a gentle, good-natured animal, although much livelier in its movements than the common ox.

Plate 24.

a. The Buffalo (*Bos bubalus*). The body of the Buffalo is full and round; neck short, head broad, horns immensely strong and bent; legs of middling length, very strong; tail rather long. Its dark-brown hair is sparse, except upon the shoulders, the front of the neck, and the tuft of the tail. This animal originated in the

East Indies; has been naturalized in Asia, Africa, Turkey, Hungary, and Italy. It makes an imposing and threatening appearance, and is an enemy not to be despised, as it is able to cope with the tiger. When tamed, it is so docile that a child may lead it; it draws immense burdens; furnishes excellent milk and savory meat. Bathing is indispensable to the domestic as well as the wild Buffalo. The American Buffalo is the Bison (*Bos Americanus*).

b. and *c.* The GOAT (*Capra domestica*) differs so much in size, color of the hair, and length and form of the horns, that it is difficult to tell whence it came. It is a very intelligent and useful animal; sure-footed and hardy, and quite at home among rocks; as in the sheep, all parts of it are useful. Goat's milk is thicker and richer than that of the cow.

d. The STEINBOCK, or IBEX (*Ægoceros ibex*) (*Capra ibex*), is one of the most perfect of goats; its manner of living, beauty of figure, and strength of limb represent the title of the goats as mountain animals. A full-grown buck is from four and a half to five feet long, two to three feet high, and weighs about two hundred pounds. Both sexes have handsomely curved horns, which bend backward; those of the male grow to three feet in length. These horns, which are very large, square in front, and marked with transverse and prominent ridges, give this goat an imposing appearance. Its color changes; in summer, its hair is short, and of a reddish-gray color; in winter, it is fawn-colored, thicker and longer. The Ibex surpasses even the Chamois in watchfulness and prudence, boldness and agility; and yet they are so much reduced in number that only a few are now found on Mt. Rosa, whilst, formerly, they roamed in numbers over the German and Swiss Alps. They keep together in small herds; lie quietly during the day, on the most precipitous and highest points of rocks; and descend in the evening to pasture on Alpine herbs.

Plate 25.

a. The Wild Goat (*Ægoceros œgagrus*) (*Capra œgagrus*). The size of the body and length of the horns of the Wild Goat are about the same as those of the Ibex, for which it is often shown in menageries; but the horns are quite different, and both sexes have a thick beard and greater variety of coloring. This Goat is found in herds on the mountains of Persia and other mountains of the eastern hemisphere. The balls, which are found from time to time in the stomach of the Wild Goat, are considered, by some tribes, as an important medicine, and are the chief object in hunting it. This is regarded as the parent stock of all the numerous domestic varieties.

b. The Cashmere Goat (*Capra Thibetensis*); the most celebrated of all for its fine wool. The whole body of this Goat, except the head and ears, is covered with long, silky hair, "under which is a delicate gray wool, about three ounces of which are obtained from a single individual; and it is of this wool that the renowned Cashmere shawls are made." The length of this animal is about four and a half feet; height, two feet; the color is either a yellowish-white, or brown, or black. The most valuable are the pure silver-white animals. It is everywhere kept in Thibet and the neighboring countries. Since 1819, it has been introduced into France; it thrives well, and furnishes a wool not inferior in quality to that of Thibet.

c. The ARGALI (*Ovis argali*) (*Ovis ammon*) is a powerful, strong-limbed Sheep, of six feet in length and four feet in height. The curled horns of the male are from three to four feet long, and weigh from thirty to fifty pounds; those of the female are smaller and straighter. A large individual of this species weighs from three hundred to three hundred and fifty pounds. It is found in Eastern Asia, and an allied species on the Rocky Mountains of America, where it lives in families. Its manners resemble those of the Chamois.

d. The Nepal GOAT (*Ovis nepalensis*) (*Capra nepalensis*) is rather smaller than the Domestic Goat; it has longer legs and shorter hair, and resembles the Sheep. Its head is homelier than that of any other kind of Goat; horns and beard generally wanting. This Goat has been known since the earliest times in its home, Upper Egypt, and can be seen in most of the zoölogical gardens.

PLATE 26.

a. The Sardinian SHEEP (*Ovis musimon*) differs from the Argali in being smaller, as well as in the smallness of the horns of the female. Its length, including the four-inch tail, is four feet; height, two and a half feet; its hair is soft, and reddish on the back and white below. These sheep live in herds of forty to fifty under the guidance of a strong wether, and pasture on the rocky mountains of Sardinia and Corsica; they are very strong, and agile in springing and climbing. Timid and shy, they have just prudence enough to avoid threatening danger.

b. and *c.* The Domestic SHEEP (*Ovis aries*) differs from the Wild Sheep by its curled hair, called wool, and by its long and pendent tail. The character of the Domestic Sheep differs also: the Wild Sheep are lively and gay; they act, in a certain degree, with consideration; while the tame Sheep is a stupid creature, indifferent to every thing, and does not even know how to help itself out of danger: it would placidly run into its own destruction, but for the shepherd and his faithful dogs. The profit derived from sheep is great: beside the flesh and skin, so much in demand, they are kept for manure and wool.

d. The Merino SHEEP (*Ovis merino*), a middle-sized, strong built animal, characterized by the length and fineness of its wool. The Merino Sheep is found in other countries beside Spain; crossings with common sheep have produced a race, for example in Germany, whose wool is said to be as fine as that of the true Merino.

PLATE 27.

Equidæ, or Horse Family. — This family comprises animals which have only one apparent toe and a single hoof to each foot; although they have under the skin spurs representing a toe on each side of their metatarsus and metacarpus. The genus *Equus* comprises all the species.

a. The HORSE (*Equus caballus*) is the largest and most beautiful of the single-hoofed animals. It is characterized by small, pointed ears, loose mane, and long, hairy tail. The varieties of the Horse are very numerous, but are all regarded as one species. The contrast between a heavy Burgundy Horse and an English Racer, between an Arabian Horse and a Scotch Pony, is very striking. All are noble, intelligent animals, deserving the love of man; but the most beautiful of them all is the Arabian Horse, illustrated on our plate; next come the English race and hunting Horses; then the Persian, Turkish, Hungarian, Spanish, &c.

The Horse no longer exists in a wild state, except in those countries where horses once domesticated have been set at liberty, as in South America and Russian Asia. These wild horses have rather gained than lost in swiftness and endurance; but their heads are thicker, and they have lost in beauty.

b. The Ass (*Equus asinus*). In order to appreciate the near relationship of the Ass to the Horse, we must not take the neglected animal as shown in our illustration for a standard. In Asia, where it originated, it is a beautiful animal: there are also fine Asses in Spain and Southern Italy, which bring nearly as high a price as the Horse. The Ass has long ears, and a tuft at the end of its tail. The Mule is the offspring of the Ass and the Horse. Although the Northern Ass is not so lively and easily guided as the Southern, he is, at least, not a stupid beast (as he is often called), but rather cunning, and merits our respect for his patience, endurance, and frugality.

c. The ZEBRA (*Equus zebra*) resembles the Ass; but is rather larger, and regularly marked throughout with black and white transverse stripes.

d. The Quagga (*Equus quagga*), of Africa, "resembles both Horse and Zebra, though differing in specific characters. The neck and shoulders are brown, striped with white; tail and legs whitish; ears smaller than in the Zebra. The voice of the Quagga is like the barking of a dog."

Plate 28.

Phocidæ, or Seal Family. — Amphibious animals whose home is in the sea.

a. The Common Seal (*Phoca vitulina*) abounds in the cool and frigid regions; its head is roundish, and doglike in form and expression; neck, short; body, elongated, muscular, and flexible; finlike feet, and toes terminated with pointed nails; length from four to six feet; color, yellowish-gray above, more or less shaded and spotted with brown, and dirty white below. The Seal is in all large zoölogical gardens, where it shows itself to be an extremely intelligent animal, easily tamed, and understanding every sign of its keeper; unfortunately, however, it cannot live long in confinement. Its food is fish, of which it eats a considerable quantity at once.

b. The Sea Bear (*Phoca ursina*) has smaller ears, and longer neck and limbs than a Seal. It might be taken for a land animal, as it crawls so quickly, that a man can escape it only by going up hill. The Sea Bear is from six to eight feet long; its body is covered with coarse, thickly-set, dark-colored hair above, and yellowish-gray below. It is described as a courageous animal, especially in defending its young. It is very serviceable to the inhabitants of Greenland, who make use of all parts of its body.

c. The Sea Lion (*Phoca jubata*), from fifteen to twenty feet long. Its skin is fawn-color, and the male has a long bristly mane, like that of a Lion. It is found in the Pacific Ocean. Some natural historians describe them as shy and timid animals, yet defending themselves bravely when driven to extremities.

d. The Walrus (*Trichechus*) of the Arctic regions is the size of the largest ox, and from fifteen to twenty feet long; has two tusks weighing from fifteen to thirty pounds; and is covered with short, brown hair: otherwise it resembles the Seals. The Walrus is stupid and lazy; but when attacked, it develops its power, and defends its young with great courage. It is hunted for its skin, flesh, fat, and tusks, which are hard as ivory.

The Sirenidæ, or Siren Family, come between the Seals and the Whales.

The Siren is a lazy, stupid animal; feeds mostly on water-plants, and seldom goes on land. One of the best known is —

e. The Manati, or Lamantin (*Trichechus manatus*); it is from nine to ten feet long, and weighs from five to eight hundred pounds. It is characterized by a movable, snoutlike upper lip. It is found in the rivers and on the Atlantic coasts of the warmest countries of America, where it is zealously hunted for its skin and its flesh.

The allied Dugong is a native of the East Indies.

Plate 29.

Balænidæ, or Right Whale Family. — "This family comprises Whales which have no real teeth; but the two sides of their upper jaw are furnished with rows of vertical horny plates, called whalebone, formed of a sort of fibrous horn, and which are fringed on their inner edges. This arrangement is adapted to the nature of the food of these Whales, which consists of small marine zoöphytes, mollusks, and crustaceans."

a. The Greenland Whale (*Balæna mysticetus*) is confined to the frigid regions, and is common to the North Atlantic and North Pacific Oceans. It attains the length of from fifty to seventy feet; the head is about one-third its whole length. From this species is obtained the flexible whalebone in slabs of from eight to ten feet in length; one Whale yielding from six to eight hundred strips on each side of the palate. A single Whale sometimes yields more than one hundred tons of oil.

b. The Sperm Whale, or Cachalot (*Physeter macrocephalus*), is seventy feet long. The head constitutes one-third of the whole animal; the upper part of this enormous head consists of large cavities, filled with an oil which becomes hardened as it cools, and which is called spermaceti. Ambergris is a concretion formed in the intestines of Sperm Whales, when affected by certain diseases. This animal has conical teeth in the under jaw, which fit into the cavities of the upper jaw. It inhabits deep, tropical, and temperate seas.

Plate 30.

a. The NARWHAL (*Monodon monoceros*) is about twenty feet long. The male has a spirally-furrowed tusk ten feet long. As far as known, this animal inhabits the northern seas. It swims in companies, and is harmless.

b. The DOLPHIN (*Delphinus delphis*) has a beaklike muzzle, and from forty to forty-seven pointed teeth on each side, both above and below. Its color is black above, and white beneath; body, from six to ten feet long. Dolphins live in communities, and are celebrated for the velocity of their movements. They are found in all seas.

The Grampus and Porpoise are nearly allied genera.

BIRDS: AVES.

Plate 1. — Birds of Prey.

Vultures. — Beak, bent, hook-like; head, either naked or covered with down; food, carrion; sight, extremely good; lazy and cowardly; they can fly very high. They inhabit warm countries, live in flocks, and are useful in eating carrion.

a. The Carrion Vulture (*Vultur (Neophron) percnopterus*) is white, with black wings; head and throat, naked, and of a yellowish color; length, not quite two and a half feet. Its young are brown. This carrion bird is tolerated in the cities of Southern Europe, and in the East, as a scavenger. The Egyptians considered it a sacred creature.

b. The White-headed Vulture (*Vultur (Gyps) fulvus*). The head and neck of this Vulture are white, other parts of the body a grayish-brown, bordering upon yellow; neck, surrounded by a collar of light-brown feathers; it measures from tip to tip ten to twelve feet. It inhabits Africa and the countries of the Mediterranean, and often wanders into Germany. It is more generally diffused than any other Vulture.

c. The Condor (*Vultur (Sarcoramphus) gryphus*) is the largest of all the birds of prey, four feet long, and having a spread of wing of ten to twelve feet. This gigantic bird sometimes soars away to the height of six miles, keenly surveying the surrounding country for its accustomed food.

d. The Bearded GRIFFIN, or LAMMERGEYER (*Gypaëtus barbatus*) is orange-color, with brown back and wings, the latter striped with white; under its beak is a tuft of bristles. It inhabits Switzerland, Tyrol, and the south of Europe; is a powerful robber, which attacks chamois, goats, sheep, &c., and has even carried off children. It measures ten feet, with spread wings, flies easily, and pounces, arrow-like, from an immense height upon the quiet pasturing animal.

e. The Secretary BIRD (*Gypogeranus serpentarius*); tarsi, extremely long; toes, short; tail, wedge-like; color, a bluish-gray, with a tuft of black feathers on the back part of the head. It is three feet long; inhabits Southern Africa. It catches serpents, lizards, &c.

PLATE 2.

The EAGLE and the FALCON (*Falco*) have a short and strongly curved bill, the latter with a distinct tooth near the point; claws, large, strong, curved, and very sharp; wings, pointed; tail, long and wide.

a. The Golden EAGLE (*Falco fulvus, Aquila chrysaëtos*). From the appearance, courage, and strength of this Eagle, it is called the king of birds. It inhabits the woods, and pounces upon hares, fawns, large birds, &c., for its prey. It builds its nest upon high trees or cliffs of rocks; its eggs, of a dull whitish color, spotted with brown, are two in number, and three inches long. The plumage of this bird is brown: the female is three and a half feet long, and somewhat larger than the male. The European Golden Eagle and the American are by some supposed to be the same species.

b. The ERNE, or great Sea EAGLE (*Falco* (*Haliaëtus*) *albicilla*); plumage, grayish-brown; tail, white. It is found over all Europe and in Greenland; is thirty-five to forty inches long; feeds on aquatic birds and fish in summer, and on all sorts of game in winter. It builds its nest upon high cliffs.

c. The Serpent EAGLE (*Falco brachydactylus*); toes and claws, short; color, brown above and whitish below; cere and feet, bluish; tail with three dark cross bands; length, two and a half feet. This bird lives in the south of Europe, and feeds on serpents.

d. The KITE (*Falco milvus*) (*Milvus regalis*) is two feet long; plumage, rust-color; head, whitish, dashed with black; tail, forked. The Kite flies slowly, turns for a long time in a circle without apparently moving its wings, and can fly very high. It builds its nest upon high trees; catches hens, geese, mice, frogs, &c., but is a lazy and cowardly bird.

PLATE 3.

a. The Common HARRIER, or HEN-HAWK (*Falco* (*Circus*) *cyaneus*). The old male is ash-gray, with white breast; female and young are dark-brown above, and white below. The Harrier is found in all Europe, North America, and Cuba. It feeds on mice and small birds.

b. The Common BUZZARD (*Falco* (*Buteo*) *vulgaris*);

legs, yellow; plumage, brown above, and spotted-white below. The Buzzard is a migratory bird; and, although stupid and lazy, it is useful, as it lives on field-mice.

c. The OSPREY, or FISH-HAWK (*Falco (Pandion) haliaëtos*), two feet long, is dark-brown above, and white below; legs and toes, greenish-yellow; bill, bluish. The Osprey lives in the neighborhood of ponds and rivers, and preys upon fish. Searching for food, it flies at moderate heights, and when it spies a fish, plunges perpendicularly into the water upon its prey, which it seizes with its strong claws. It builds its nest upon high trees; it is said to be very mild in its disposition.

The American Fish-Hawk is the *P. Carolinensis.*

d. The Noble, or ICELAND, FALCON (*Falco islandicus*), of Northern North America and Greenland, is about two feet long; the plumage, white; the upper parts with regular transverse bands of brown, and the under parts with a few narrow stripes of the same color. This species is the most highly esteemed by falconers.

e. The GOSHAWK (*Falco (Astur) palumbarius*) is two feet long. It is grayish-brown above, and white below, when old; when young, it is reddish-white below, with dark spots. It is spread over Europe and North America, and is very detrimental, as it seizes birds, pigeons, and partridges, even in flight.

PLATE 4.

a. The Peregrine FALCON (*Falco peregrinus*) is about a foot and a half long; wings, fifteen inches; upper parts, bluish-ash color, with bands of brownish-black; under parts, yellowish-white, with dark, circular spots, and bands of black upon the sides, under tail coverts and tibiæ; quills and tail, brownish-black; bill, light-blue, and the legs and toes yellow. This Falcon is spread over the northern parts of the globe, and is a dangerous robber of pigeons, ducks, &c. The European Peregrine Falcon was formerly much used in falconry.

b. The HOBBY (*Falco (Hypotriorchis) subbuteo*), one foot two inches long; wings and tail, of the same length; is bluish dark-brown, with thighs and rump fawn-color. It is very bold, and chases larks.

c. The KESTREL (*Falco tinnunculus*) (*Tinnunculus alaudarius*) is of a beautiful brownish-red, and spotted above; the male has gray head and tail; this well-known bird builds in towers and on rocks. It feeds on mice and small birds.

d. The SPARROW-HAWK (*Falco (Accipiter) nisus*), of Europe, is eleven to twelve inches long, and the wing about seven inches. It feeds upon small birds, mice, and other small animals. It may be seen day after day in the same place, watching for its prey.

e. The Singing FALCON (*Falco musicus*) inhabits the southern parts of Africa, and is characterized by its singing, instead of croaking like other Falcons.

PLATE 5.

The Owl Family. — This family comprises all the nocturnal birds of prey. They are characterized by a large head, large eyes, curved bill, nearly concealed by bristle-like feathers; large ear-cavities, and a catlike expression. This family is represented in all parts of the world. About one hundred and fifty species are known, some forty of which belong to America. With the exception of the Great-eared Owl, they are very useful birds, destroying a great number of mice. They build in ruins, towers, and high trees.

a. The Great-eared OWL, or Eagle OWL (*Strix bubo*) (*Bubo maximus*), of all the northern countries of Europe, is from twenty-one to twenty-four inches long; wing, about sixteen inches. It is distinguished from all other owls by its large size and conspicuous ear-tufts; its plumage is various; its food consists of mice, snakes, frogs, and poultry. This Owl generally builds its nest on a branch not far from the trunk of the tree; lays from three to six eggs, almost globular and white.

b. The Long-eared, or Horned, OWL (*Strix otus*) (*Otus vulgaris*), is fourteen inches long, and has very long ear-tufts. It perches on a low tree or shrub from which it darts into the woods when disturbed. Its plaintive cry is repeated at intervals. It seldom builds a nest for itself, but rears its young in those which it finds.

c. The Tawny OWL (*Strix (Syrnium) aluco*). The pupil of this Owl is dark-brown; plumage, sprinkled; male, gray; female, rust-color.

d. The White, or Barn, OWL (*Strix flammea*); plumage, gray, mixed with black and white above; rusty-yellow, or whitish with black spots below. It is sixteen inches long, the wing thirteen inches. This Owl is found in all temperate North America, and frequently resorts to barns and old buildings in search of rats and mice.

e. The Little Night OWL, or Naked-footed OWL (*Strix*

passerina); plumage, yellowish-brown, with white spots. It lives in old buildings, is attracted by candlelight, and, on account of the piteous noise which it makes in the night, is considered by superstitious people as the harbinger of death.

PLATE 6.

The Shrike Family.—LANIUS. The birds of this family have a very strong bill, hooked at the tip; both mandibles are notched, and there is a distinct tooth in the upper one. They not only catch insects, but mice and small birds, and have the singular habit of impaling upon twigs and thorns those which they cannot swallow at once. They cān imitate the sounds of other birds.

a. The Great, or Ash-colored, SHRIKE, or BUTCHER BIRD (*Lanius excubitor*); above, gray; below, white; wings and tail, black. Although only about nine inches long, it attacks larger birds, even partridges.

b. The Red-backed SHRIKE (*Lanius spinitorquus*); head, gray; wings and back, reddish-brown. It imitates the melodies of other birds. It is an enemy to the May Beetles, impaling a number before it begins to eat them. It is found in Europe and Asia.

c. The Lesser SHRIKE (*Lanius minor*) resembles the Great Shrike, but has a black forehead and fawn-colored belly. It builds its nest of odoriferous plants, and upon a strong branch.

SCANSORES, or CLIMBERS: with toes, two before and two behind.

The Parrot Family comprises birds which have a thick, rounded bill, hooked at the tip, and the base covered with a soft skin. Most of them are adorned with gorgeous plumage, and many can be trained to imitate the human voice, which makes them objects of particular attention. The Parrot family are all children of the tropical climes, and are so well known by their brilliant dress and aptitude to learn, that a farther description is unnecessary. They are known as parrots, macaws, cockatoos, and parroquets.

d. The Red and Blue MACAW (*Psittacus* (*Ara*) *macao*) has a long, pointed, wedge-like tail, and unplumed cheeks. It inhabits the Antilles and South America.

e. The Alexander PARAKEET (*Conurus Alexandri*) is green; neck and bill, pink. It is found in the East Indies, and is seen in all menageries and zoölogical gardens.

f. The Black COCKATOO (*Psittacus* (*Calyptorhynchus*) *Temminckii*) is grayish-black, with tuft on the head, and red on the tail. It is a native of New South Wales; feeds on insects, seeds, and larvæ.

PLATE 7.

a. The Common Gray PARROT (*Psittacus erythacus*) is gray, except the tail, which is red. It is one of the most tractable and also the most costly of Parrots; it is a native of Western Africa.

b. The Sulphur-crested COCKATOO (*Psittacus* (*Cacatua*) *sulphureus*) is a fine-looking bird, which can erect and depress its crest at pleasure. It is a native of India and Australia, where it forms one of the most beautiful ornaments of the woods.

c. The TOUCAN (*Ramphastos*) has an enormous bill, bent near the end and indented along its edges; however, it is very light; tongue, fringed on both sides; plumage, black; breast and neck, variegated. It inhabits the warm regions of South America. The Toucan lives on fruits and insects, which it throws into the air and then catches as they descend, and thus swallows them more easily.

Woodpecker Family.—PICUS. This family comprises birds characterized by a straight, sharp bill, adapted to cutting into bark or wood; and by a long tongue, armed with barbs toward the tip, and capable of great extension. They have stout feet, long wings, ten primaries, and twelve tail-feathers. Woodpeckers feed upon the larvæ of insects, which they secure by introducing their tongue under the bark of trees or into crevices, also into holes which they themselves have made: the larvæ adhere to the viscid substance with which the tongue is covered. They are common in both hemispheres.

d. The Black WOODPECKER (*Picus martius*). The male of this Woodpecker has red on its head; the female, red on the back of its neck.

e. The Green WOODPECKER, or POPPINJAY (*Picus (Gecinus) viridis*), is green, with red on the head. It is smaller than the Black Woodpecker.

f. The Greater Spotted WOODPECKER (*Picus major*). Its back is black; rump, carmine-red; the male has red on the back of its head. It is the most gayly dressed of its family.

g. The Lesser Spotted WOODPECKER (*Picus minor*) is black, with white bands; the male has a red spot on the top of its head. It is very useful in destroying a great number of insects.

PLATE 8.

a. The Median Spotted WOODPECKER (*Picus medius*); back and tail, black; breast and neck, pale yellowish-brown; crown, carmine red.

b. The WRYNECK (*Yunx*) can turn its neck on all sides; is about the size of a Lark; mottled-brown above; yellowish-white, with brown spots below. It builds on high trees, and feeds on tree-insects.

c. The Common NUTHATCH (*Sitta Europæa*) is ashy-blue above, rusty-brown below; a black line runs through the eye. It is a lively bird, which climbs a tree quicker than a Woodpecker, and industriously draws out insects from cracks in its bark. It breeds in hollow trees, and closes the opening of its nest with clay, so that it only can slip in and out.

d. The KINGFISHER (*Alcedo*), a beautiful bird, whose color changes from blue to green; its belly is rust-color. This shy and timid bird lives near ponds and rivers, where from trees, poles, and stones it sits watching for fish, which constitutes its food; at the proper moment it plunges into the water, seizes the fish, which it turns in its beak to swallow head first. The nest is made in a hole at the end of a tube, which it digs in a high bank of a stream to the depth of three feet; the eggs, six in number, are pure white.

e. The European BEE EATER (*Merops apiaster*) is eleven inches in length; brown above, throat yellow, belly verdigris-green; its home is Asia, Africa, and the south-east of Europe. It lives on insects which it catches as it flies, and destroys many bees; it digs its nest on the shore like the Kingfisher; it is one of the most beautiful of European birds.

f. The Common Hoopoe (*Upupa epops*) has a long, thin beak, slightly bent, and an upright crest upon its head. It feeds on insects and larvæ. Its nest, of rotten wood and cow-dung, is found in hollow trees and holes of walls. The peculiarity of this bird is, that the female, during the time of breeding, secretes a liquid from its rump gland which has the smell of ammonia.

Plate 9.

a. The Common Creeper (*Certhia familiaris*) is five and a half inches long; the color, dark-brown above, each feather having a white streak, and the rump is rust-color, the under parts white. It runs up and down trees, and feeds on insects. The female breeds twice a year in the hole of a tree.

b. c. d. The Humming Birds (*Trochilus*) belong exclusively to America, and are numerous in the hot regions. The feet of the Humming Birds are very small, wings long and narrow, tail broad. The bill is thin, sharp-pointed, straight or curved; plumage, beautiful and variegated. The tongue, which is split almost to the base, forms a sort of tube, which it protrudes into flowers to obtain its food, which consists of insects and honey. About four hundred species are known.

e. The Raven (*Corvus corax*) is two feet long; plumage, of metallic lustre. It is found in America, Asia, and Africa. The Raven is rather shy and cautious, but can be tamed; is attracted by shining things, which it steals. The Raven learns to repeat words, and lives to a great age. Carrion is its favorite food; but it attacks hares, partridges, and field-mice.

f. The Carrion Crow (*C. corone*) resembles the Raven in color, but is smaller. Its shyness and cunning are well known. Notwithstanding its propensity to scratch and pull up corn, it is a very useful bird in destroying a very great number of grubs destructive to the crops.

g. The Rook (*C. frugilegus*), of Europe, is nineteen inches long; black, with a purplish gloss. Its food is worms and insects. The Rooks build socially upon trees, so that sometimes fifteen or sixteen nests are found upon one tree, where these birds are in continual dispute about place and material for building.

Plate 10.

a. The Hooded Crow (*C. cornix*); head, throat, wings, and tail, black; other parts, gray.

b. The Jackdaw (*C. monedula*). The color is blackish, with silver-gray neck; under parts, ash-gray. These birds are thievish, easily tamed, and like to build on towers.

c. The Jay (*C. (Garrulus) glandarius*) is fourteen inches long; upper wing coverts, blue and crossed with white; its voice is harsh, but it learns to imitate sounds; food, insects, worms, acorns, hazel and beech nuts, &c. The Jay is found in North and Temperate Asia and Europe.

d. The Nut-cracker (*C. (Nucifraga) caryocatactes*);

bill, long and straight; plumage, dark-brown, with white spots. It inhabits forests, and eats the seeds of the Siberian Pine, also eggs. It is smaller than the Jay, and not so common.

e. The Mountain Rook (*C. Alpinus*) is black; bill, thin and yellow; feet, red. This Rook is found in great numbers in the Alps. It can be tamed, and has the same inclination to steal shining things as the Jackdaw.

f. The Cornish Chough (*C. (Coracia) gracula*) is also black; its bill is longer than that of the Mountain Rook, and, like its feet, coral-red. It inhabits the Alps, and is a shy and unsocial bird.

g. The Magpie (*C. (Pica) melanoleuca*); back, lustrous-black; upper part of the wing and belly, white; tail, long and pointed. This is a cunning, thievish bird, easily tamed, and learns to speak some words. It lives on insects, worms, fruit, mice, and birds; it has the name of robbing the nests of partridges, ducks, and hens, and eating their young. Its nest, made of brush and thorns, is an almost impregnable fortress.

Plate 11.

a. The Roller (*Coracias*) is of a bluish-green; bill, cinnamon-color, sharp-edged, and bristled at the corners; feet, yellow; a bird of passage. It often seizes frogs by the thigh, strikes them on the earth, and then swallows them. The Roller, on account of its beautiful plumage, is sometimes called the German Parrot. It lives in Europe and Africa.

b. The Bird of Paradise (*Paradisea apoda*), peculiar

to New Guinea; it is about the size of the Robin; rich maroon-color; the crown and neck, yellow; the throat and around the bill, emerald-green. The sides of the tail have a handsome-plume of long, loose feathers of a light-yellow hue, and on either side of these are two shafts nearly two feet long. These birds live in flocks of thirty to forty; feed on insects which they catch while flying, and are easily caught when their feathers are disarranged by a storm.

c. The Golden-crested WREN (*Rupicola*). The male is orange-color, with a large crest; lives on fruits, and scratches in the earth like the hens. It builds a nest of small brush, and lays two eggs.

d. The Golden ORIOLE (*Oriolus*) is yellow, with beautiful black wings. Its artistic nest is basket-like, and hung on the forked ends of a branch; its favorite food is cherries.

e. The Purple GRAKLE (*Gracula* (*Quiscalus*) *versicolor*), of the United States, is of a lustrous black; head and forward parts glossed with purple; but the female is gray. Its length is about fifteen inches. The Grakle lives mostly on insects, except in harvest-time, when it eats grain.

f. The MINA BIRD (*Gracula religiosa*), black, with violet hue; behind the eye is a naked flap of skin; its bill and feet are yellow. It inhabits the East Indies, and feeds on fruit. The Mina is about the size of a Jackdaw. It becomes tame and familiar, and learns to repeat words more distinctly than the Parrot.

g. The CUCKOO (*Cuculus*). The bill of this bird is slender, curved, and narrow toward the end. It is very shy, and seeks thick foliage where it sits uttering the peculiar note from which it is named; it feeds upon insects and eggs. The Cuckoo does not build a nest, but lays in the nests of other birds.

Plate 12.

The Lark Family. — ALAUDINÆ. The family of Larks have a thin conical bill, not as long as the head. They are distinguished by an awl-like spur on the hind toe; they build their nests on the earth; they have a peculiarly measured pace, and live on seeds and insects.

a. The Field, or Sky LARK (*Alauda arvensis*). This Lark is, next to the Nightingale, the sweetest songster in Europe, and charms every lover of nature; its dress is an unassuming grayish-brown above, and yellowish-white below. Formerly the Lark was brought to market, by thousands, for the table.

b. The Wood LARK (*A. arborea*) is a little smaller than the Field Lark; has a shorter tail, generally with white tips and a white spot on the cheeks. The nest is built on the earth; the food is the same as that of the Field Lark.

c. The Crested LARK (*A. cristata*) is distinguished by a pointed crest on the head; the color is like the other larks, except that the lower wing coverts are rust-red. Like the Domestic Sparrow, this Lark lives near human habitations. Its note is pleasant, and flute-like.

d. The STARLING (*Sturnus*) is about the size of a Thrush; its color is violet and greenish-black, spotted with white or pale-yellow. This is a pleasant, lively bird, which imitates the melodies of other birds. It has a strong, straight bill, and feeds on seeds, berries, and insects. It is found in Europe, Asia, and Africa.

e. The Common DIPPER (*Cinclus aquaticus*) is dark-brown above, yellowish below; breast, white. This bird seeks woody countries in the neighborhood of cool brooks, and lives on aquatic insects, snails, and small fishes. It lives in Germany, and its simple song is often heard on a sunny winter's day.

f. The Song THRUSH (*Turdus musicus*). That of the United States excels all other American birds in the sweetness and softness of its notes. Its color varies a little from the European, which is also noted for its song. Its food consists of insects, larvæ, and berries. The genus *Turdus* has the bill stout and shorter than the head; wings, pointed and long.

PLATE 13.

a. The Missel THRUSH (*T. viscivorus*), of Europe, is olive-brown above, the under parts of the wings white, breast spotted. It is fond of the mistletoe; it inhabits the pine woods of all Europe. In spite of its charming song, it is killed in fall for its flesh, which is considered a delicacy.

b. The Field-fare THRUSH (*T. pilaris*) is a native of the north of Europe, goes to the South in October, and returns North in April. It feeds on worms, insects, and berries; color, chestnut-brown above; head and lower part of the back, gray; breast, rusty, with dark spots; belly, white. Its flesh is savory, and much esteemed.

It is said that in East Prussia alone, over six hundred thousand pairs of the Field-fare Thrush are shot yearly for the market. They nest in the northern countries of Europe and Asia, and keep together in large flocks; their food is that of other Thrushes, though they prefer juniper-berries.

c. The Ring Thrush (*T. torquatus*) is black, extremities of the quills white, a large half-moon-like white patch on the breast. Flocks of three to four thousand lead a quiet and lonely life in high mountain forests.

d. The Blue Thrush (*T. cyaneus*). The male is of a dark slate-blue color, with beautiful azure-blue wings, and the tail black, bordered with blue. It inhabits the southern countries of Europe, and is admired for its fine, loud, and clear notes.

e. The Blackbird (*T. merula*) is of a fine black color, with bright yellow bill. The female is brown. In Central Europe, this is the first bird to celebrate the return of spring.

f. The Silkstart (*Ampelis garrula*), called also the Bohemian Chatterer, or Waxwing, is of a brownish-ash color; tail-feathers, slate, with a terminal yellow band; head and throat marked with black, the secondaries with red horny tips. The Cedar Bird of North America is much like the Silkstart, and both are distinguished by the silky and soft tints of their plumage. Their food consists of insects and berries.

Plate 14.

The Cross-bill Family has thick, strong mandibles, curved and overlapping at the points. The seeds of pine cones are their favorite food.

a. The Common CROSS-BILL (*Loxia curvirostra*) is six and three-quarter inches long. The old male is dull red; wings and tail, blackish-brown. The female is dull greenish-olive; rump and crown, yellow, beneath grayish. It builds a thick, warm nest upon the pine, and lays three eggs.

b. The Cherry FINCH (*Loxia* (*Pinicola*) *enucleator*) has the upper mandible bent over the lower one like a hook; white bands on the wings; young males, yellow or yellowish-red; older ones, nearly carmine-red; the females are never red. They inhabit the North, and live like the Cross-bills.

c. The BULLFINCH (*Loxia* (*Pyrrhula*) *rubicilla*); head, wings, and tail, changeable black; upper part of the body, a bluish-gray; belly of the male, cinnabar-red; that of the female, dingy reddish-gray. The Bullfinch is well known in all Europe; goes from north to south in autumn, and is a quiet, confiding bird, and often caged. It lays four or five eggs, and breeds twice a year. It feeds on seeds, grains, and berries.

d. The Green FINCH, or Grosbeak (*Loxia* (*Fringilla*) *chloris*) is of a yellowish-green; edge of wings and tail, bright yellow; not rare. It is found in North Africa and in Asia as well as in Europe. It feeds on seeds containing oil.

e. The Common GROSBEAK (*Loxia* (*Coccothraustes*) *vulgaris*) appears clumsy and heavy, but can fly well. It has a black throat, reddish breast, and is otherwise brown and gray. This bird builds its nest in gardens, and eats the kernels of cherries. The Grosbeak is at home in the temperate zones of Europe and America.

f. The Yellow BUNTING (*Emberiza citrinella*); the

head and lower part of the body, beautiful yellow; back, rusty, with black stripes; a very common bird. It builds in hedges and bushes, and breeds twice a year.

g. The Garden BUNTING (*E. hortulana*); beak, flesh-color; head and back of the neck, grayish; is in all parts of Central Europe, where millet, its favorite food, is found.

PLATE 15.

a. The Cirl BUNTING (*E. cirlus*); front of the neck, yellow; wings, brown; female, with brownish spots. It is a rare and handsome bird; breeds once a year, and in hedges.

b. The Snow BUNTING (*E. nivalis*) is six and three-quarters inches long; the wing, over four inches; tail, short; colors, black, brown, and white; in winter, white beneath; head and rump, yellowish-brown; back, brown. Snow Buntings move in flocks, and inhabit the northern parts of both hemispheres, and feed on seeds and insects.

c. The Common SPARROW (*Fringilla domestica*); upper parts, brown, with dark spots; lower parts, light-gray; throat of the male, black; of the female, gray; old sparrows breed three times a year, young ones twice. Their food, in spring, consists of insects; in cherry-time, of cherries; in autumn, of grains. Sparrows are cunning, cautious birds; very useful, as they destroy an enormous quantity of insects.

d. The CHAFFINCH (*F. cœlebs*); tail, greenish; wings, with two bands, one white and one yellow on each wing; male, with bluish-gray head and wine-colored breast; female, brownish-gray head and reddish-gray breast. These passenger birds leave Central Europe in October, and return in March and April: the males arrive first, the females follow in flocks by themselves. The Finch builds a conical nest upon a tree, and breeds twice in a year. It is a useful bird, and its song is very fine.

e. The Mountain FINCH (*F. montifringilla*) is dark above, with orange-yellow brêast; the male and female differ in color. It builds in thick branches; lives on insects and seeds.

f. The Snow FINCH (*F. nivalis*); its upper wing and outer tail-feathers are white; back, brown; under parts, grayish-white. It inhabits the high mountains of Central Europe where the eternal snows begin, and builds in crevices of rocks.

PLATE 16.

a. The GOLDFINCH (*F. carduelis*); brown; belly, whitish; bright red about the head; wings, black and yellow; tail, black, with white edges. The Goldfinch is very intelligent, and much liked as a cage-bird. Its pleasant song is full of variety and change. It feeds mainly on seeds.

b. The CANARY BIRD (*F. canaria*). This bird was originally gray above and greenish-yellow below; its color has changed by confinement. It was brought from the Canary Islands some three hundred years ago. Its song and docility are generally known.

c. The Brown LINNET (*F. cannabina*) takes a high rank among seed-eating birds; is heard the whole year in Central Europe. Its back is brown. In the old male, the crown and breast are blood-red. It is most beautiful in spring, when attired in its wedding-dress. It is a sweet songster, and bears captivity very well; found in Europe, from Norway to the Mediterranean.

d. The LINNET (*F. spinus*); plumage, greenish; under parts, pale-yellow; crown and throat of the male, black. It is much liked for a cage-bird, and lives twelve years. It feeds on the seeds of the fir, birch, and alder.

e. The Yellow LINNET (*F. citrinella*); tail-feathers, black, with light edges; plumage, yellowish-green; neck and throat, grayish. It lives in the southern part of Europe.

f. The Common BUNTING (*Emberiza miliaria*) resembles the Lark in color; it is a bird of passage. It is spread over all Europe; it lives on the ground, and feeds upon grains and insects.

PLATE 17.

The Warbler Family comprises a large number of small and interesting birds, characterized, in part, by a conical, slender, or depressed bill. This family is represented in all parts of the world, and embraces many of the sweetest songsters. They live on insects, berries, and fine seeds, and are all birds of passage.

a. The NIGHTINGALE (*Sylvia* (*Luscinia*) *philomela*) begins the list, and stands at the head of sweet and celebrated songsters. Its simple dress is reddish-brown above, whitish-gray beneath. The Nightingale delights us with its melodies in quiet spring nights, and stops singing toward midsummer. Its food consists of worms, insects, larvæ, and berries. Its nest is very simple; it lays once a year from four to six eggs. The Nightingale is found in Europe, Asia, and Africa.

b. The Blue-throated REDSTAR (*Sylvia suecica*); tail, dark-brown and red. The male has a fine blue throat and breast, with or without spots; the female has no blue on the breast. The male has a peculiarly clear, whistling note. Its nest, in which it lays from four to five eggs, is artless. The Redstar is a native of Europe.

c. The BLACK CAP (*Sylvia atricapilla*) is grayish above; the male has a black, the female a yellowish-brown, crown. This interesting and agreeable songster is found in all Europe, except the extreme north, and particularly in the gardens and woods of Germany.

d. The White-throated WARBLER (*S. cineraria*); ash-gray above; below, whitish; has a white line on the tail-feathers; it is the enemy of insects, caterpillars, and larvæ. It is a good songster.

e. The Greater PETTYCHAPS (*S. hortensis*); above, grayish; tail and wings, brownish; body, whitish. This is one of the best of songsters. It inhabits the warmer parts of Europe; feeds on insects and berries.

f. The Lesser White-throated WARBLER (*S. garrula*); plumage, similar to the preceding, from which it is distinguished by its tones of clapp-clapp, which it from time to time mingles with its song; plumage and food, the same as the Pettychaps.

g. The Chiff-Chaff WARBLER (*S. hippolais*); above, olive-green; below, sulphur-yellow. It puts its nest, which is surrounded by white birch-bark, upon young fir-trees, or in forked twigs several feet above the ground. It sings finely; but cannot bear confinement. It is found in all Europe.

Plate 18.

a. left. The Robin, or Redbreast (*S. (Erythacus) rubecula*), is of a brownish hue, with an orange-red breast. Its fine song sounds somewhat melancholy in the evening. It builds its nest in holes or trees, and lays from five to seven eggs. The Robin is well known in the Old World. The American Robin is the migratory Thrush (*Turdus migratorius*); is a much larger bird, and belongs to an entirely distinct family.

a. right. The Winchat (*S. (Saxicola) rubetra*); brown above; throat and breast, yellowish; root of tail, white.

b. right. The Fire-crowned Gold Crest (*S. (Regulus) cristatus*); above, greenish; crest, orange and yellow. It is a very active bird. Its nest is built with an opening on the side. The female lays, the first time, from eight to eleven, the second time from six to nine, eggs, scarcely larger than a pea. It is a native of Germany, and very much like the Golden-crested Wren of the Northern United States.

b. left. The Reed-Warbler (*Sylvia turdoides*); above, rusty-gray; below, dingy yellowish-white; wings, short; tail, long and rounded. It lives in reeds and bushes near the water.

c. left. The Common Wren (*S. (Troglodytes) parvulus*) is nearly five inches long; the wing, over two inches; the color above, reddish-brown, barred with dark-brown; under parts, brownish-gray. The Wren is a gay, lively little bird. It feeds on insects and larvæ.

d. left. The Common REDSTART (*S.* (*Ruticilla*) *phœnicura*) has a black throat, and orange-red breast and tail. This is one of the prettiest and liveliest birds of the forest. It is common in Europe. North America has an allied species.

d. right. The White WAGTAIL (*Motacilla alba*); around the eye, side of the neck and belly, white; top of the head and throat, black; back, ash-gray. It is a lively bird, and constantly moving its tail. The Wagtails keep socially together, and confide in man. As soon as the cold weather commences they go off, and return in March as early messengers of spring. They build near the water, in hollow trees and holes of the shore. They breed twice a year, and lay six to seven eggs the first, and five to six the second, time.

e. The Yellow WAGTAIL (*M. flava*); olive-green above, beautiful yellow below. It lays four to six white eggs, speckled with light brown.

PLATE 19.

Parus, or Titmouse Family, comprises only small, active birds, which may well be called the mice among birds. They are insect-eaters; but their strong, short bills enable them to eat hard-shelled seeds, which they hold with their toes. Their feet are short and strong, with bent toes; they are good climbers, and often hang on thin twigs with their head downward. The plumage of the Titmice is very soft, and some of them are finely colored.

a. left. The Greater Titmouse (*Parus major*); above, dingy olive; below, yellow; head and throat, black. This Titmouse brings up from ten to twelve young ones, and destroys an immense number of insects. When confined with other birds, they attack them, split their heads, and eat their brains.

b. The Blue Titmouse (*P. cœruleus*); wings and tail, blue; back, olive-green; belly, yellow. This is a neat little bird, full of droll manners, and is found throughout Europe, except the far North. It lives on insects, larvæ, and eggs.

c. left. The Cole (*P. ater*); head and neck, black; back, blue-gray; cheeks, white; found in pine woods of Northern North America, Europe, and Asia.

d. left. The Crested Titmouse (*P. cristatus*) has a fine-pointed crest on the head. It exclusively inhabits the firs of its native land, and makes great havoc among insects.

e. left. The Marsh Titmouse (*P. palustris*) is the liveliest and funniest of all Titmice, and surpasses the others in climbing. Its crown is black; upper body, grayish; throat, blackish. It lives in marshy places, and builds its nest in old willows.

f. right. *Hirundo, or Swallow Family.* — Bill, short; wings, very long; tail, generally forked. They catch insects while flying, and are birds of passage.

a. right. The Chimney Swallow (*Hirundo rustica*); plumage, steel-blue above; forehead and throat, chestnut-brown; belly, reddish-white. It is uncommonly quick in flight; builds in houses, and is everywhere protected by man as a friend.

b. right. The House Martin (*H. urbica*); above,

blue-black; throat and belly, white; feet, feathered nearly to the claws. These Martins build their nests of mud and clay, side by side, on the outside of houses. The nests are so strong that they are not easily broken.

c. right. The Sand MARTIN, or Bank SWALLOW (*H. riparia*); grayish-brown; throat and belly, white; it nests socially in holes in banks. It is the smallest of the swallows, and the least numerous. This Swallow perches on trees and bushes, and builds its nest on the banks of rivers. In Germany, they are mostly found near the Rhine, Danube, and Elbe.

d. right. The GOATSUCKER (*Caprimulgus*); bill, short, triangular, and bristled; plumage, variegated and soft. It lives in forests or woods, feeds on insects, has a gentle flight, but flies only in the night. The Goatsucker lays two eggs on the heath, without building a nest. It does not suck the milk from Goats, as its name would imply.

PLATE 20.

Columbidæ, or Dove Family. — Bill thin, slightly bent at the tip; feet, short; wings, long and pointed; tail-feathers, twelve or fourteen; plumage, generally of a metallic lustre. Pigeons live in pairs, build nests upon trees and in the holes of rocks, lay two eggs at a time, and breed several times in a year. The young are at first fed by the old ones with macerated food from their own crops. Seeds constitute their chief nourishment. They are spread over the whole earth. The very large species are limited to the southern zones.

a. The Domestic PIGEON (*Columba livia*, var. *domes-*

tica). The soft skin, in which the nostrils are situated, is whitish; plumage, bluish-gray; neck, glossy, with greenish and bluish hues; rump, white; pupil, red; and a double black band upon the wings. This Pigeon is found wild in some parts of Africa. The fostering care of man has produced a great number of varieties.

b. The Tambourine DOVE (*C. tympanistria*) has feet covered with long feathers; it derives its name from the drumming noise which it makes. It is from fifteen to sixteen inches long.

c. The Short-tailed DOVE (*C. livia, var. brevicauda*); smooth head, and large red, naked circle about the eye. This Dove pounces down, like lightning, in a straight line, at the same time turning itself over and over, and more rapidly as it approaches the earth.

d. The Dwarf PIGEON (*C. nana*) has curled feathers, like a ruffle, on the breast, and a short bill.

e. The Fantailed PIGEON (*C. livia, var. laticauda*) has a handsome, upright, outspread tail, consisting of from twenty-eight to thirty feathers: it belongs to the Domestic Pigeons.

f. The Nicobar PIGEON (*C. (Calænas) nicobarica*). This Pigeon, in regard to form and manner of living, bears much resemblance to a hen: it is a native of Nicobar and the Moluccas; it keeps on the ground, and builds under bushes.

PLATE 21.

a. The Wood PIGEON (*C. œnas*) has a red bill with yellow point; plumage, above gray, with incomplete bands on the back; below, wine-color.

b. The Powter, or Cropper-Pigeon (*C. livia,* var. *gutturosa*), can inflate the elastic skin of the neck to an enormous size. There are many varieties of this kind of Pigeon.

c. The Passenger Pigeon (*C.* (*Ectopistes*) *migratorius*) is seventeen inches long, and the wing eight and a half inches: its twelve-feathered and wedge-like tail shows that it can fly well; and indeed this Pigeon undertakes journeys of many hundred miles from its home in North America. "Sometimes they fill the air like a cloud, and thus continue to pass for a whole day." They have been known to destroy entire fields of grain, and break down trees upon which they were roosting in great numbers. They build their nests of dry sticks and twigs; some forty to fifty nests are found upon one tree. Plumage, bluish above, purplish and white below. The female is smaller, and in color duller, than the male.

d. The Rock Pigeon (*C. risoria*). It is rust-color, with black trimmings, and becomes very tame. It was brought from India. Its original color was much lighter and more pinkish, with a black half-circle on the back of the neck.

e. The Common Turtle Dove (*C.* (*Turtur*) *auritus*). This gentle and beautiful bird is kept as a pet, especially among country people in Germany, who superstitiously consider the Turtle Dove as the conductor for all human ills. Its plumage is of a tawny slate-color, with black feathers on the sides of the neck, in the form of a ring. It is named from its cooing note, which sounds like turtur. It inhabits Europe, Asia, and Africa, and builds its nest in thick underbrush.

f. The Great-crowned Pigeon (*C. (Goura) coronata*) is found only in hot climates. It grows as large as a turkey.

g. The Common Quail (*Coturnix vulgaris*) is rust-red, with angular-shaped spots of black. The male has a dark-brown, and the female a whitish, breast. It is from ten to twelve inches long, and the wing from four to five inches. The note of the male sounds like dic-cur-hic. The female lays from eight to fourteen pure white eggs; and she, alone, takes care of her young. The Quail is used in Asia as the fighting-cock is in England. In Italy, they are caught in great numbers for the market.

Plate 22.

a. The Ptarmigan (*Tetrao (Lagopus) mutus*) has the legs feathered to the claws, which are black and strongly bent; plumage in winter, white; upper tail-feathers, black; in summer, more or less marked with brown and yellow; wings, belly, and feet, white.

b. The Black Cock (*Tetrao tetrix*); tail, forked and curled outward; the male, two feet long, is black, with a metallic lustre; the female, smaller, is tawny, with black bands. The Black Cock is found in Alpine countries; is fond of birch woods; goes far into the North. It is useful in destroying insects, and for food.

c. The Cock of the Wood, or Capercailzie (*T. urogallus*); male, black, sprinkled with white, green lustre on the breast, a feathered beard, and brown wings; female smaller, and rust-color, with cross bands. This Cock is as large as the Turkey, being one of the largest of the Gallinæ. Its flight is low, rustling, and of short duration; sight and hearing, very sharp. It lives in high mountainous woods; on the ground in the daytime, and on trees in the night. Its food consists of insects, berries, herbs, buds, and foliage. During pairing-time, in March and April, the Cock keeps up a peculiar sound from two A.M., until twilight, while marching around his tree in a dandified manner, when he can be easily shot; at other times, he is cautious, and not easily taken. He has from eight to ten hens in pairing-time, after which he leads a lonely life, and does not allow another Cock on his premises. The hen lays from seven to ten eggs on the bare earth; sits four weeks. This Cock is found in Europe and Asia.

d. The Common PARTRIDGE (*Perdix cinerea*); face and throat, a beautiful reddish-brown; back, a mixture of ash-gray, black, and yellow; on the neck are fine, black, wavy lines. The male and female remain together until death. The female lays from twelve to twenty-two eggs, in a simple hollow on the ground; breeds in May or June. The young ones run immediately, often with the shell sticking to them; they remain with the old ones until the next spring, forming one family. Both sexes care for their young, protecting them under their wings in bad weather. The Partridge flies heavily, but is a good runner, and is easily tamed.

e. The Red PARTRIDGE (*P. rubra*); cheeks and throat, pure white, surrounded by a dark band; breast, ash-gray, with black, red, and white spots; belly, lighter; back of the head, tawny-red; pupil and bill, red. It is a native of France and Italy. Its character and manners differ from those of the Partridge, inasmuch as it is untamable, and the male takes no care of the young.

f. The Mountain GROUSE (*T. saxatilis*) is mostly ash-gray; throat, white, bordered with black; bill and feet, red; belly, fawn-color; handsomely marked feathers. This Grouse is found in the East, and in the south of Europe. It is a domestic bird in the Grecian Islands.

g. The PINTADO or GUINEA FOWL (*Numida meleagris*), is found wild in the marshes of Africa, in flocks of from two to three hundred. It has a naked head, with a reddish-brown callosity in the form of a helmet; color of plumage, blue-gray, speckled with white spots. It is kept with other poultry on account of its delicious flesh; it has a disagreeable note; it lays from seventy to seventy-five eggs during the summer.

h. The Common FOWL (*Gallus domesticus*), descended from the Jungle Fowls of India, is spread over the whole earth; and, through the fostering care of man, its varieties are now almost endless. The cock has many hens of which he takes care, and for whose protection he fights bravely. The hen lays from eighty to ninety eggs yearly.

PLATE 23.

Phasianidæ, or Pheasant Family. — The male, as with most other birds, is larger than the female, and his plumage is more brilliant. Either the whole head, or a part of it, is naked; or it has a feathered crest. The tail of the cock is often much developed, and, with some, can be spread like a fan.

a. The Silver PHEASANT (*Phasianus* (*Gallophasis*)

nycthemerus) has a black tuft on the head ; male, white above, with fine zigzag dark lines ; violet black on the under parts ; female, reddish-brown, with green spots ; the belly crossed with black lines.

b. The Golden PHEASANT (*Thaumalea picta*), " so remarkable for its magnificent plumage, has a golden-colored crest; the neck, orange, speckled with black; the back, green; the rump, yellow; the lower parts and wings, red, the latter with a blue spot; and the long tail, brown, spotted with gray." The Golden Pheasant comes from East India and China. It is much more delicate than the other pheasants, and it requires particular care to bring up the young. The cock puts on his gala dress in his second year. This Pheasant often attains the age of twelve years.

c. The Argus PHEASANT (*Argus giganteus*) is five feet, three inches long; female, two feet, two inches; central tail-feathers and wings, very long, and the latter covered with ocellated spots, so that, when the wings are spread, the appearance of this bird is splendid. Its home is Sumatra.

d. The PEACOCK (*Pavo*) has the head crested; tail, short; rump-feathers, on the contrary, excessively elongated and adorned with eyes. Its splendid plumage and power of raising its rump-feathers are well known. The white is also very beautiful. Peacocks shed their feathers, except those of the crest, every year. They live to be twenty-five years old; their voice is disagreeable; home, the Indies. Alexander the Great is said to have introduced this bird into Europe.

e. The Impeyan PHEASANT (*Lophophorus Impeyanus*) has a crest like that of the Peacock; plumage, brilliant red, green, blue, yellow, with metallic lustre about the head and neck; lower part of back, white; tail, reddish-brown; belly, black. The male is one of the most brilliant of birds. The color of the female is a brownish-gray, marbled with yellow.

f. The Common TURKEY (*Meleagris gallopavo*); head and upper part of the neck, naked; from the forehead an elastic, fleshy appendage; tail, long and spreading; plumage, copper-bronze, with black edgings. The Turkey is about four feet long. It is a native of the United States, and its offspring are spread over both hemispheres. The male weighs from eighteen to twenty pounds, and more. Its flesh is everywhere esteemed as a delicate article of food.

PLATE 24.

Otidæ, or Bustard Family. — The Bustards have strong feet, with three broad-soled toes; large, broad wings, and short, round tail, consisting of twenty feathers; body, too large and heavy for easy flight. Bustards live on seeds and insects. They are distrustful, and flee the approach of man.

a. The Great BUSTARD (*Otis tarda*); legs, long, and feet three-toed; tail, of twenty feathers, which can be spread like a fan; wings, short; the upper part of the body, reddish, with black waving lines; male, adorned on both sides of the head by a feathery beard. The Bustard is four feet long, and weighs from twenty-four to thirty pounds. It is a shy and cautious bird, and runs with outspread wings when chased; it can, however, fly high and easily for a long time. It is seen in Europe in flocks of from fifty to one hundred. It feeds on grain, green seeds, and insects, and lays from two to three eggs. Its flesh is good for food.

b. The CASSOWARY (*Casuarius Indicus*), of the Indian Archipelago, is about five feet high. It is a strong, stout bird, and more awkward than the Ostrich, which it resembles in manner of living. Plumage, black; head and neck, naked and blue; the flesh on the sides of the neck, red; a horny helmet on the crown; wings furnished with some barbless stems; feet, three-toed. The Cassowary feeds on fruits and grains.

c. The Two-toed OSTRICH (*Struthio camelus*) is black, with white tail and wing-feathers; the plumage consists of soft, polished feathers, which are longer on the wings, facilitating only the running of the animal, as it cannot fly. This Ostrich is the largest of birds, and the fleetest of all animals; it is from seven to eight feet high, and weighs one hundred pounds. It can strike dangerously with its strong feet, and throw large stones far behind it. It lives on grains and fruits; but swallows stones, leather, and similar substances. In the time of breeding, one male is found with four or five females; all lay in one nest, which is scooped out of the sand. The ostrich eggs are not left to hatch in the sun, as has been stated, but are brooded at intervals by the hens, and sometimes by the cock. These eggs weigh three pounds each, and are savory. The flesh of this bird is edible; its skin is worked into leather, and its plumes form an article of commerce in Africa.

d. The Three-toed OSTRICH (*Rhea Americana*). The American Ostrich of South America is distinguished from the African species by having three toes, armed with nails; color, gray; wings, lighter than the back; tail-feathers, wanting. The male has black feathers about the neck. It is about six feet long. These Ostriches live in flocks of thirty to forty on open plains, and are easily tamed when young.

Plate 25.

Phœnicopteridæ, or Flamingo Family. — This family comprises birds with very long legs and necks; toes, fully webbed; bill, bent in the middle, and the edges indented.

a. The Flamingo (*Phœnicopterus antiquorum*) is five feet long, pale rose-color; wings, carmine; feet, red; tail, black. The young are dingy white, with brown legs and reddish wings. The Flamingo is common in the warmer parts of America and Europe. Its food is insects, mollusks, and fish.

b. The White Stork (*Ciconia alba*); three and a quarter feet long; white, with black coverts; bill and feet, red. The Stork is everywhere at home in the Old World, and welcome in Europe, where he appears alone in March, and afterwards brings his mate. Both leave again in September to winter in Africa and Spain. Their food consists of mice, serpents, frogs, &c. They often build their large nests, to which they return year after year, on chimney-tops. The female lays four to five eggs.

c. The Black Stork (*C. nigra*) is of a brownish-black color, with metallic lustre; its breast and belly are white. In size, and manner of living, it resembles the white Swan; but it feeds more on fish, and builds on high trees.

d. The Marabou STORK (*C.* (*Leptoptilus*) *marabou.*) There are two kinds of giant-like Storks, one from the tropical regions of Africa, the other from India. They are furnished with a large appendage under the throat, somewhat resembling a sausage. The beautiful plumes, called Marabouts, are taken from under the wings of these birds. Color, black or brown above, and white below: head and neck covered with down.

e. The Common HERON (*Ardea cineraria*), found in all Europe, is three feet long, with a blackish tuft hanging from the back of the head; color above, ash-gray; below, white, with black spots. Its food consists principally of fish. It builds on high trees, and lays from three to four eggs. The young remain a long time in the nest.

f. The Purple-Breasted HERON (*A. purpurea*), of Southern Europe, is three feet long; plumage, bluish-gray above, purple below; crest and occipital feathers, dark-brown.

PLATE 26.

a. The Night HERON (*Ardea* (*Nycticorax*) *grisea*), is one foot, eight inches long; ash-gray above; whitish below; crown and back, blackish; it has three long, white feathers on the back of the head. Night Herons are found in America, Asia, and Africa.

b. The Little BITTERN (*A. minuta*), of North America, is thirteen inches long; head above, and back, dark-green; other parts, mostly cinnamon-color. The nest is built on low bushes; eggs, three to four; dull yellowish-green.

c. The Common BITTERN (*A. stellaris*) is two and a

quarter feet long; the color is brownish-yellow, varied with dark-brown; head, black, glossed with green; is found among reeds, and has a peculiar, loud note.

d. The Common CRANE (*Grus cinerea*) is three feet, ten inches in length; back of the head, naked and red. Cranes are found in America, Europe, and Asia. They wander in large flocks, and form two lines, meeting in an angle in front. They fly so high, that, although they can be heard, they are not seen. The Crane is known to be watchful and cautious; it has a loud voice, feeds on grains, green seeds, peas, &c., also worms, mussels, and frogs. The female lays two eggs in her nest, which is made of reeds. The young birds can run so quickly that man cannot catch them.

e. The IBIS (*Ibis religiosa*); bill, feet, wings, and the naked part of the head and neck, black. The Ibis is about the size of a common Hen, and was worshipped and embalmed by the ancient Egyptians.

f. The SNIPE (*Scolopax*) is about thirteen inches long, and has twelve tail-feathers, and a very long bill; it is reddish-brown, with fine, black cross-lines above, and yellowish-white below. It is everywhere, and sought for by the hunter, as an article of food; even the intestines, with their contents, are eaten as a delicacy.

g. The Common SNIPE (*S. gallinago*) is found in all countries where there are low, marshy lands, and is much esteemed for its delicate meat. Its tail has fourteen feathers.

h. The Common LAPWING (*Vanellus cristatus*); feet, red; a tuft of feathers hanging from the back of the head; back, dark-green, with a purple lustre; breast, black; belly, snow-white. The Lapwing is very common in the meadows of all Europe. Its spotted eggs are much esteemed by the gourmand.

Plate 27.

a. The Ruff (*Machetes pugnax*). The plumage of the Ruff varies very much; the male has a feather collar about his neck in summer. The female and young never have a collar. These birds always keep near the sea and large lakes. In spring, the males fight continually among themselves; notwithstanding this, they fly in company, but recommence their fights as soon as they alight on the ground. The Ruff is accidental on Long Island, North America, and much resembles that of North Europe.

b. The Water, or Marsh, Hen (*Gallinula chloropus*); above, olive-green; below, gray; crown, red; feet, green; found in Europe. The Marsh Hen, or King Rail, of the Atlantic and Pacific coasts of North America in the warmer parts, is seventeen inches long; under parts, rufous-chestnut.

c. The Corn Crake (*Crex pratensis*), of Europe, Greenland, and accidental in the United States, resembles the Lark in color. It is improperly called the King of the Quails, from the circumstance of being often found with them in harvest time.

d. The Jacana (*Parra*); wings, spurred; toes, long, slim, and armed with long, sharp claws. It inhabits the ponds and marshes of hot climates; runs quickly over water-grasses, and makes much noise.

Gulls (*Larus*). — Bill, strong; tail, nearly even; colors, light; and head, white.

e. The Black-headed Gull (*Larus rudibundus*); wings, white with black border; back or mantle, silver-gray; lower body, white; bill and feet, red; head and throat, dull-brown in summer; white, with dark spots on the ear, in winter.

f. The Black-backed Gull (*L. marinus*) is thirty inches long, and the wing nine inches; mantle, blackish slate-color; wings, ornamented with white; feet, flesh-color.

g. The Herring Gull (*L. argentatus*) is twenty-three inches long, the wing eighteen inches; the head, neck, under parts, rump, and tail, white; back and wings, light blue-gray.

Plate 28.

a. The Common Tern (*Sterna hirundo*) is white, with ash-gray back and wings; bill, red, straight and pointed; tail, forked; crest, black; feet, red. This bird flies almost all day long, and generally does not swim. It darts down upon small marine animals, and is found along the sea-coasts.

b. The Jager (*Lestris*) is much like the Gull; bill, indented, bent at the point; it lives on fish, insects, worms, and carcasses, the first of which it does not catch itself, but takes from the Gulls, to which it gives chase; color, white brownish-gray.

c. The Petrel (*Procellaria*); bill, short, slender, and bent at the point. It is six inches long; plumage, rusty black and white. This bird is found far out at sea, a proof of its endurance in flying; for it seldom or never swims. Before a storm, it seeks protection on rocks, or on ships; for this reason, seamen consider it the harbinger of evil.

d. The ALBATROSS (*Diomedea*); bill, very strong, the upper mandible curved at the point; feet, three-toed, with large webs; color, generally white, though it varies much. The Albatross is as large as a swan. It inhabits southern seas, builds its nest on earth-hills, and lives on fish; eggs, savory; flesh, unsavory.

e. The Great White PELICAN (*Pelecanus onocrotalus*); bill, very long, and hooked at the end; under the lower mandible, and opening into the throat, is a very large, naked, and elastic pouch. The old birds are pale-pink, the young ones whitish. The Pelican is six feet long, and weighs from twenty to twenty-five pounds; it is found in the Mediterranean sea, and can fly extremely high; its note resembles the braying of an ass; it can swallow a fish of several pounds' weight, and retains a store of provisions in its pouch. Eggs, from two to five; breeding-places, marshy islands.

Cygnus, or Swan Family. — Bill, of equal breadth; neck, extremely long and graceful. The Swan prefers the water to the land, and feeds on marine plants and insects.

f. The Common SWAN (*Cygnus olor*) is four and a half feet long; bill, reddish-yellow; plumage, white; feet, black. The Swan is found wild everywhere in Europe, and on sea-coasts, rivers, and lakes. In autumn, flocks of forty to fifty collect and go southward. The Swan swims proudly, but can fly well and high. The female lays from six to eight eggs in a miserable nest, which she uses year after year.

g. The Singing SWAN (*C. musicus*); bill, yellow at the root, and black at the end; plumage and feet, like the preceding. It inhabits the northern portions of

America, Europe, and Siberia. It has a sonorous note, which has given rise to the fairy tales of the singing Swan.

h. The GOOSE (*Anser*); bill, orange-yellow, strong, and narrower at the point than at the root. The legs of the Goose are set in the middle of the body, which accounts for the Goose walking much easier than the Duck, or the Swan. Geese are found on water and land, and live on water-grasses and grain. This is the parent of our domestic Goose.

PLATE 29.

a. left. The Field GOOSE (*Anser segetum*). Its black bill is orange-color in the middle; wings, longer than the tail. This Goose is found in the north of America, Europe, and Asia. It is a careful and watchful bird; migrates, under a leader, in large flocks.

b. left. The BERNACLE (*A. bernicla*); head, neck, bill, and wings, black; about the neck, a white ring. It breeds in the polar zones, and comes accidentally into the temperate zones. It is found in immense flocks on the French and Danish coasts in winter.

The Duck Family (*Anas*) is distinguished from the Goose by its flat and equally broad bill, by its horny tongue, and by its short neck.

a. and right *b.* The Eider DUCK (*Anas* (*Somateria*) *mollissima*). Two naked lines run from the fawn-colored bill to the forehead; the top of the head is black. The male is whitish; belly, tail, and lower wing-feathers, brownish; the female, brown, spotted with black. This bird inhabits the extreme north of both hemispheres, lives near the sea, and never goes farther south than the Hebrides. It swims, flies, and dives well, and is much sought for its eggs, and more for its down, which is of the finest and best quality known. Five pounds of eider down are sufficient to fill a good-sized bed.

d. The Harlequin Duck (*A.* (*Clangula*) *histrionica*); plumage of the male, bluish-gray, with black and brown spots, and two white rings about the neck; the brilliant spots wanting in the female. Bill of this Duck, very small; tail, pointed. It measures seventeen and a half inches.

e. The Tufted, or Velvet Duck (*A.* (*Oidemia*) *fusca*), has a white patch round the eye, and white on the wings; male, black; female, rusty. It inhabits the north of America, Europe, and Asia, and is accidental upon the Swiss lakes.

f. The Common Duck (*A. boschas*); head and upper parts, mostly green, with a violet gloss; it has a white ring around the middle of the neck; fore part, and sides of the breast, brown. It is generally diffused, and everywhere well known. This is the original of the common domestic duck.

g. The Common Sheldrake (*A.* (*Tadorna*) *vulpanser*); head and neck, green; back, black; under parts, yellowish-red; bill, red; upper parts of the female, lighter than those of the male; lower parts, the same color. The Sheldrake is twenty-six inches long. It is found in the temperate zones of America and Europe.

h. The Cracker (*A.* (*Dafila*) *acuta*); above and on the sides, ash-gray, finely waved with black; lower parts, white; head, dark-brown; wings of the male ornamented with green; of the female, with red; central tail-feathers, black, and much elongated. The Cracker, or Pintail, is found in the northern part of both hemispheres.

Plate 30.

a. The Green-headed GOOSANDER (*Mergus*); bill, much serrated, long and narrow; the head and neck of the male, black, with a greenish gloss; lower parts, whitish salmon-color; neck, pure white; female, less brilliant; is found as far north as Lat. 54°; common to both hemispheres.

b. The Crested GREBE (*Podiceps cristatus*); bill, straight, slender, and pointed; toes, each separate, and surrounded by a web. In the spring, its head is covered with tufts; plumage, above, dark-brown; below, brilliant silver-white. The skin of the Grebe is used for fur. Its food consists of frogs, fish, and insects. Nine species, varying in length, belong to North America.

c. The DIVER (*Colymbus*), of the northern regions, is as large as a Goose; its bill is about four inches long; head and neck, brilliant black; throat and back of the neck, banded with white; back, black, spotted with white; lower parts, white; feet, fully webbed; tail, short and rounded.

d. The GUILLEMOT (*Uria*); color, black; a white patch on the wing; bill, straight and pointed; wings, short; feet, red. The Guillemot lives on fish, and swims and dives well. The female lays but one egg, and that of considerable size; she is so zealous in breeding, that she often allows herself to be taken on the nest. Flesh, eggs, and feathers used particularly by the inhabitants of the Faroe Islands.

e. The Great Auk (*Alca impennis*) is two and a half feet long; bill, flattened and grooved; upper parts, black; lower parts, and a spot over the eye, white; its wings are too small for flying. It inhabits the polar regions, and is seldom seen.

f. The Puffin (*Mormon fratercula*) has a very high, short, red and yellow bill, obliquely grooved on the sides; upper parts, crown, and neck, black; lower parts, white; cheeks, light-gray. The Puffin is an Arctic bird; it makes its nest in a burrow, which it digs to a considerable depth. The flesh and large eggs of the Puffin are good for food, and its skin is used for fur.

g. The Penguin, or Manchot (*Aptenodytes*); bill, straight; upper mandible longer than the lower; feet, four-toed; tail, short and stiff; wings, very small, and fringed with hornlike scales. This bird, of the cold regions of the southern hemisphere, swims continually, flying under water with its wings, and goes on shore only to lay its eggs. It is about the size of a Goose, black above, and white below.

SERPENTS.

Plate 1.

Serpents. (*Serpentes*), (*Ophidia*). — Serpents have a long cylindrical body, and are generally covered with scales, which are largest under the belly. Although they have no feet, they move with extreme rapidity, by means of their spine, which consists of many vertebræ, often more than two hundred; and the numerous ribs extending nearly the whole length of the body, with the vertebræ, making up most of the skeleton. The heart is provided with two auricles; the lung is single, and extends nearly the whole length of the body; the tongue is long, soft, very distinctly forked, and can be stretched out very far, and is altogether harmless. The voice is only a hissing. The mouth is extremely dilatable, so that they can swallow animals much thicker than themselves; during the very slow process of digestion, they fall into a torpid state. Serpents cast their skins, at least, once a year, and attain a great age. Some serpents lay their eggs in sand or manure; others, especially venomous snakes, are viviparous. In cold countries the serpent falls into a torpid state in winter. They are dangerous to man, on account of their size and ferocity, and more especially by the deadly poison contained in a gland behind and above the hook-like and retractile teeth. There are serpents which are not poisonous, and which may be eaten. The greater part live on the land; a few only live in the water.

a. The BOA (*Boa constrictor*). The head distinct from the body, tail provided with a small hook on each side of the anus, jaws armed with teeth, and rudiments of hind limbs, or spur-like appendages. It is from twenty to thirty feet long, and the most terrible of all serpents. It not only attacks man, but large animals. Winding itself around its prey, it crushes the bones, moistens with saliva, and then swallows it whole. When satiated, the Boa falls into a torpid state, when it is easily killed. Its skin is variegated; it is an inhabitant of the hot regions of South America. The Python lives in Africa.

b. The RATTLESNAKE (*Crotalus horridus*); tail, flat and provided with a rattle, which consists of movable horny rings, with which they make a peculiar noise when alarmed. This poisonous snake of America is six feet long, but less dangerous than is generally represented by travellers. It is a lazy animal, which moves out of man's way, if not provoked. Its food consists of hares, birds, and water-animals, which, as they swim easily, they catch in ponds and rivers. The Rattlesnake is eaten by the Indians, after the head is taken off.

PLATE 2.

a. The Spectacle, or Cobra de capello, SNAKE (*Naja tripudians*) is distinguished by a black line upon the neck, resembling the figure of a pair of spectacles. It is from two to four feet long, and the most poisonous snake of the Old World; but is frequently tamed by the jugglers of India, who extract its poisonous fangs.

b. The Common VIPER (*Vipera berus*); brown, with a double row of transverse spots on the sides, and dark crescent-formed spots upon the head. Its length is about two feet; it is found in all Europe, but particularly in woody and mountainous countries. The bite of this serpent is most dangerous in warm countries; at times, causing speedy death. Unprovoked, it is harmless.

c. The Ringed SNAKE (*Coluber natrix*) is steel-colored; the head of the male is encircled by a yellow necklace; the belly is whitish, with square spots; it is from three to four feet in length. Its food consists of moles, mice, frogs, and small fish. It is found over all Europe. It swims well, and can remain for a long time under water; it climbs trees, and remains in holes during the winter in a torpid state.

d. The Esculapian SNAKE (*C. Esculapii*); above, brownish; below, yellowish. It is five feet long, and can be tamed; found in the southern part of Europe.

PLATE 3.

a. The Smooth SNAKE (*C. lævis*); scales on the back, smooth; upper part of the body, reddish-brown, or green, with two rows of irregular dark spots running lengthwise the body. It is not poisonous, but easily excited, and bites fiercely; found in Germany.

b. The Yellow Water SNAKE (*C. flavescens*) is five feet long; brown or grayish-brown, belly whitish-yellow; scales on the back, smooth; those on the belly, rough.

c. The Water Snake (*Hydrus*); found only in hot climates; lives in rivers and seas; is very poisonous; its tail is compressed and flat.

d. The common blind worm, or Glass Snake (*Anguis fragilis*). The body of this reptile is covered with overlapping scales; tail, long and shining, and easily broken; its color is reddish-brown, with elongated black lines on the back; it grows to the length of one and a half feet, and frequents sunny places. As it renders itself useful by consuming snails, insects, and worms, it ought not to be destroyed. At present, it is classed with the lizards, on account of the breast-bone. It is not blind.

Plate 4.

Lizards (*Saurians*).— These are scaly, long-tailed reptiles, generally having four feet furnished with nails. The mouth is large, and armed with teeth. The young slip out of the thin, calcareous egg in perfect form. Most lizards live on land; crocodiles generally live in the water.

a. The Alligator, or Cayman (*Alligator* (*Crocodilus*) *lucius*). The muzzle of the Alligator is broad and obtuse. Its color is dark yellowish-brown above, changing into a lighter yellowish below, with single dark spots and lines. It is found in the Southern States of America, and is sometimes dangerous to man, and attacks boats. It devours all kinds of animals,— fish, muskrats, dogs, ducks, &c. It attains the length of fourteen to fifteen feet.

b. The Nile Crocodile (*Crocodilus vulgaris*) is of a greenish color, with black cross-lines; when full grown, it measures from twenty to thirty feet. The shields, or scales, are so hard on its back, that a ball cannot penetrate them; but the Crocodile is easily wounded underneath, where its shields are soft. It inhabits the Nile and other large rivers of Africa; lies hidden in ambush, among the reeds, and attacks the animals coming to drink. It is as timid on land as it is courageous in the water. Crocodiles attain the age of a hundred years.

PLATE 5.

a. The CHAMELEON (*Chamæleo Africanus*) is a singular animal, with long legs, angular head, large eyes, long and prehensile tail. Its lungs are very large, and can be strongly inflated, so that their red color is seen through the body, and changes to black, yellow, or spotted; the blood being more or less pushed towards the skin. The eyes move independently, one of the other, one looking up while the other looks down. The Chameleons are slow, lazy animals, which hold themselves upon the trees, where they remain immovable. Their food consists of insects, which they take up with their long and sticky tongue; they are found near the Nile, and in Southern Spain.

b. The Common LIZARD (*Lacerta viridis*); back, reddish-brown or green; abdomen, greenish-yellow. Lizards are common in dry places, under hedges and piles of stone. They are quick and agile in their movements, and are useful in destroying a great number of insects.

c. The Nimble LIZARD (*L. muralis*) is dark-gray, brown, or green above, with longitudinal black lines;

red or white, with black spots, below. It is found in Central Europe.

d. The LEGUAN (*Iguana*); body and tail, covered with small scales; along the back is a range of spines; the throat has a pendent and compressed dewlap. Its color is greenish-yellow; tail, banded with brown; its length, from four to five feet; its home is in the warmer countries of America. The Leguan is quick and nimble, lives on fruits and insects, and is generally found on trees. Its flesh and eggs are used for food.

e. The BASILISK (*Basiliscus*) is entirely scaled, and the back furnished with a range of spines. This animal has no similarity to the fabulous Basilisk. It lives on trees; but goes also into the water, and is harmless.

f. The Flying DRAGON (*Draco volans*) has a fold of skin, supported by extending ribs, which forms a sort of wing, and acts like a parachute in sustaining it, as it jumps from tree to tree, — often a distance of from twenty to thirty feet. The color of the upper parts is green; the wing, brownish, with dark cross-lines. This little, harmless animal lives on trees in the East Indies, and hunts insects.

PLATE 6.

SALAMANDER (*Salamandra*). — The body of the Salamander is lengthy, tailed, and four-footed; toes, without nails; teeth, in the back part of the jaws. Its food consists of insects, worms, and snails.

a. The Common SALAMANDER (*Salamander terrestris*); body, covered with warts; tail, round; behind the ears are two large glands filled with holes. It is black, spotted with yellow, and from six to seven inches long. It is found in Central and Southern Europe, in dark, moist places, particularly in mountainous countries. It moves slowly, and, like the toad, goes out at night. The female brings forth living young.

b. The TRITON, or WATER NEWT (*Triton aquaticus*) has small ear-glands; tail, compressed. It is not so warty as the Salamander. It lives in the water, and swims about quickly, but comes out in autumn to hide itself in the crevices of rocks and holes for its winter's sleep. It has an astonishing tenacity of life, freezing in the ice without being hurt. It also has a wonderful power to reproduce a lost part; a limb may be removed, and it will grow again. The Newt lays single eggs, which develop a tadpole, as seen in our illustration.

c. The PROTEUS (*Proteus*); body, eel-like; fore feet, short and far from each other; the fore feet have three toes, and the hind ones only two; the snout, smooth and obtuse; both jaws, furnished with teeth; it has three spiracles on each side the neck, and these are covered with three bright red branchial tufts, into which the blood from the head flows. This peculiar animal is found in the waters of Adelsberg Cave and Carniola, Zirknitz, and Sittlich.

d. The Gilled SALAMANDER (*Siren lacertina*) is from twenty to twenty-four inches long. Its color is black, with light spots; abdomen, purplish. It has an eel-like body, front feet, and spiracles and tufts like the Proteus. It feeds on worms and insects; lives in mud, and is common in the ditches of rice-fields, especially in South Carolina.

Plate 7.

Frogs and Toads. — The changes which the Frog undergoes, until it comes to its perfect state, are very remarkable. The female lays all her eggs at once; these form a kind of skin in toads, or bunches in frogs (see Figs. *a.*, *b.*, &c., of this Plate), and are found only in the water. The egg is a slimy ball, with a black point in the middle, which is the embryo. This develops itself into the tadpole, a fish-like creature without feet, and with a long tail. Behind the head are three branchial orifices, with tufts, through which the blood passes. After some days, the skin grows over these orifices, and there remains only a small hole on the left side. Then the extremities begin to appear, the posterior first; the tail is gradually absorbed, lungs take the place of gills, and the perfect frog is formed (see Plate). These are called Batrachians.

The Toad (*Bufo*); body, short and thick; back, full of warts; glands behind the ears; hind legs, shorter than those of the Frog. In hot countries, there are species from eight to ten inches long.

a. The Common Land Toad (*Bufo cinereus*); dingy-gray, with large brown warts; when full grown, it measures from five to six inches in length, and is very thick-bodied. It lives in dark, wet places, in gardens and old buildings, and is nocturnal. Its food consists of insects and worms. Toads lay their eggs in two strings of forty feet in length; number of eggs, twelve hundred. They live to a great age.

b. The Red, or Crossed, Toad (*B. calamita*); two

inches long; back, olive-brown, with reddish-brown warts; the middle of the back, a long yellow stripe. In spring, it resorts to the pools to lay its eggs; at other times, it keeps in dark, damp places.

c. The Great Brazilian TOAD, or PIPA (*Pipa Americana*); the front toes are long, round, and equal, back toes united by a web; body, covered with rough warts. The Pipa is six inches long; lives in Brazil and Guiana. Its flesh is eaten by the negroes. As soon as the eggs are laid, the male rubs them on the back of the female; the swelling skin form cells around the eggs, in which the tadpoles are developed in about three months, during which time the female remains in the water.

d. The French FROG (*Rana esculenta*); upper parts, green; lower parts, white; all spotted with black; three yellow lines run down the back. Its color is handsomest in the spring; later in the season, it changes to a bluish. These Frogs live in ponds, which they leave for short distances, and jump into the water again at the approach of danger. They pass the winter in the mud, and rouse from their winter sleep about the first of May. They lay their eggs in June; but their young are not perfectly formed until autumn. They feed on insects. Their flesh is delicate.

e. The Green TREE-FROG (*Hyla arborea*) is of a beautiful green above, and white below, covered with small warts. The upper and lower parts are divided by a yellow line, with a black edge. The male makes a loud noise in the breeding season, and when the weather is about to change. In some country villages, they are kept in glasses as weather prophets.

PLATE 8.

TURTLES (*Testudinata*). — Turtles are distinguished from all other animals by having their body enclosed in a shield, which consists of two parts, the upper called *carapace*, the lower, *plastron*. From this shield protrude head, feet, and tail, as movable parts. The jaws are covered with a horny substance, and destitute of true teeth. Turtles are very tenacious of life, and indifferent to wounds; they can live a long time without food; they move and grow very slowly, but attain a great age. Some species weigh from seven to eight hundred pounds. They lay their eggs in the sand to be hatched by the sun. The flesh of many kinds is savory. They subsist on snails, worms, insects, small fish, and some kinds of vegetables.

a. The Giant, or Green, TURTLE (*Chelonia Mydas*); the back shield has thirteen plates; full grown, it weighs five hundred pounds or more. It is much esteemed for food; and great numbers are caught on shore at night, as they come there in troops to deposit their eggs. They are found in the warm parts of the Atlantic coast of America.

b. The Land TORTOISE (*Testudo Græca*); shell, high and arched; legs and feet so arranged that the body is raised free from the ground. It feeds on plants, insects, and worms; it has been known to live twelve days after its head was cut off. Kept in a garden, one Turtle lays from thirty to forty eggs, toward the end of June, in a pile of sand; the young are not developed until the end of September. This Tortoise inhabits the coasts of the Mediterranean.

c. The Carret Turtle (*C. imbricata*); the plates overlap like tiles; they are transparent, and beautifully marbled with yellow, red, and brown; it is also known under the name of Hawk's-bill, or Tortoise-shell Turtle. It inhabits the warm parts of the Atlantic, and is nearly as large as the Giant Turtle. Its eggs are used for food; but its flesh is considered unhealthy.

d. The Marsh, or River, Tortoise (*Emys.*) The toes of this Tortoise are separate, and armed with sharp nails. The carapace is black, the plates arranged in rows. It is common in rivers and ponds.

FISHES.

Plate 9.

Fishes have cold blood, and breathe by means of gills. The difference of form in this class of animals is best seen by our illustration. Most fishes are scaly, some are naked, others spinous, and others mailed. Instead of limbs, as in the higher class of animals, fishes have fins as instruments of motion. Their senses of smell, sight, and hearing depend on organs analogous to those of other vertebrates. The nostrils are simple cavities at the end of the muzzle. The organ of hearing consists of a sac enclosed in the bones of the head. The tongue is generally immovable, covered with a rough skin, or armed with teeth, and therefore not to be considered as an organ of taste. The organs of digestion are similar to those of the higher class of animals. The jaws, tongue, and sometimes the palate, are armed with teeth, which are not for chewing, but seizing, the food. The females have two long sacs, which, in the spawning season, are filled with eggs; the males have similar sacs, which contain the so-called milt. The female lays her eggs all at once, attaching them to stones and aquatic plants, after which they are fecundated by the milt of the male. Fishes produce a far greater number of eggs than any other vertebrates, often millions; for example, the Cod is said to produce some 9,000,000. The gills lie on each side of the neck, and consist of fringes suspended on arches, and traversed by innumerable blood-vessels. In some species, the great opening of the gills is closed by means of the branchial membrane. Fishes keep currents of water flowing over their gills, where the blood, which is continually sent from the heart, is purified. Fishes die when the gills dry up, and the blood can no longer circulate. As the lungs are wanting, fishes have no voice. The true function of the so-called swimming-bladder is not known; it is probably a rudimentary lung. The skeleton of fish is not always of hard bone, but cartilaginous, and hardens with age. Fishes migrate from seas to rivers to lay their spawn. They are voracious, and feed mostly on smaller members of their own class; although a few feed on vegetable matters. Fishes are everywhere an important article of food; and fishing is the chief occupation of many inhabitants of coasts and islands. They are divided into Bony and Cartilaginous. Most fishes are oviparous, some are viviparous.

CARTILAGINOUS FISHES.

Shark Family, Squalidæ. — Several species of this family are viviparous; others produce eggs covered with a horny substance.

a. The White SHARK (*Squalus* (*Carcharias*) *vulgaris*) has five gill-openings on each side; the body is long; skin, rough like a rasp; behind the eyes are two orifices through which it spirts water. The jaws are furnished with six rows of sharp, saw-like teeth. This Shark is one of the most voracious of animals, not only swallowing fish, but man, in whose neighborhood it lurks. Sharks are sought for their liver, from which excellent oil is made; and for their skin, which is used for the covering of trunks.

b. The Hammer-headed SHARK (*S.* (*Zygæna*) *malleus*); head, flattened horizontally, with the sides laterally extended. This peculiarly formed fish attains the length of twelve feet, and is extremely bold and voracious. It is found in the Mediterranean Sea, and the Atlantic Ocean.

c. The SAW-FISH (*S.* (*Pristis*) *antiquorum*); snout, long and depressed, armed on each side with pointed spines, flattened like teeth; this is a terrible instrument, with which they attack even whales.

PLATE 10.

Ray, or Skate Family. — Body, flat and almost entirely surrounded by fins; eyes and nasal orifices, above; mouth and branchial openings, below. The tail resembles a handle; mouth, armed with pavement-like teeth. Skates live on the bottom of the sea, and feed on other animals; fully grown, they weigh from one to two hundred pounds. The flesh is eaten, and the liver used for oil; its egg-cases are brown, and rectangular with the angles extending into points.

a. The Eagle SKATE (*Raja* (*Myliobatis*) *aquila*); tail, with one fin; teeth, like pavements; found in the Mediterranean Sea, and growing to a great size.

b. The Electric SKATE (*R.* (*Torpedo*) *marmorata*); skin, smooth, of a yellowish-red color, and spotted. This fish weighs from fifteen to twenty pounds, and has the peculiar quality of an electric machine. If one attacks it, the arm receives an electric shock which benumbs it for some time. This Torpedo lives on the European coast, particularly that of the Mediterranean.

c. The Spinous RAY (*R. rubus*) is provided with bent thorns; found in the North Sea.

The Lamprey Family. — *Petromyzonidæ;* seven branchial openings on each side, and the vertebræ cartilaginous and very soft. The tongue in these animals moves backward and forward like a piston, enabling them to produce a vacuum, and thus attach themselves to stones and animals, and bore into the largest fish.

d. The LAMPREY (*Petromyzon marinus*); mouth, furnished with several circular rows of teeth; length, from two to three feet; color, green, marbled with brown. The Lamprey is found in the European seas, particularly the North Sea; in spring, it ascends far up the rivers. Its flesh is pleasant to the taste, but not very digestible.

e. The Nine-eyed LAMPREY (*P. fluviatilis*) has only one row of teeth in its mouth; its two back fins are separated; its length, not more than from twelve to fifteen inches; back, blackish; sides, yellowish. They live in European rivers; are eatable in winter only.

f. The Fringed-lipped LAMPREY (*P. Planeri*); length, eight to ten inches; back fins united; this fish is likewise found in European rivers.

g. The SANDPREY (*Petromyzon branchialis*) is found mostly in slimy brooks, and resembles the preceding.

Plate 11.

a. The Sea-owl, or Lump-sucker (*Cyclopterus lumpus*) makes use of the fins beneath its body to fix itself to stones and other objects. It inhabits the North and Baltic Seas. Pennant states, that, upon putting one into a pail of water, it adhered so firmly, that he lifted the whole pailful, — several gallons, — by taking hold of the fish by the tail.

b. The Sea-devil, or Common Angler (*Lophius piscatorius*); head, very broad and frog-like. The whole animal seems to be nothing but head and tail; mouth very large, and armed with three rows of teeth below, and two above. The chin has a thread-like beard. Color above, brownish; below, whitish. They are found in the North and Mediterranean Seas, and are two to six feet long. They are seldom eaten.

c. The Sturgeon (*Acipenser*); mouth lying on the under side, small and toothless. Sturgeons resemble sharks; but the body is furnished with rows of single, bony plates. The snout projects far over its small mouth. They inhabit the seas, but ascend far up into the rivers, attain a great size, and often weigh from nine hundred to one thousand pounds. The flesh is savory. From their roe the well-known caviare is made, and isinglass is prepared from their swimming-bladder.

d. The Common Sturgeon (*Acipenser sturio*); skin, rough, furnished with five rows of pyramidal plates. The Sturgeon inhabits lakes and seas of many countries, from which it ascends the rivers to spawn in the spring.

The flesh somewhat resembles veal, and is eaten fresh, salted, or pickled. Caviare is an important article of commerce in Russia.

e. The Great STURGEON (*Acipenser huso*); skin smooth, with rows of plates, which are smaller on the sides; color of the back, dark; sides, bluish; belly, whitish. When fully grown, it is about twenty-four feet long, and sometimes weighs two thousand eight hundred pounds. The sturgeon-fishery is very important on account of caviare and isinglass.

f. The STERLET (*Acipenser ruthenus*) is only three feet long, and is found in the Caspian Sea.

TRUNK-FISH (*Ostracion*); body enclosed in a hard coat of mail, from which only the tail and fins protrude as movable parts.

g. The Four-horned COFFER, or TRUNK-FISH (*Ostracion cornutus* (*quadricornis*), is four-cornered, and has two long horns before the eyes, and two under the tail. It attains the length of from eight to ten inches, and lives in warm seas.

h. The PORCUPINE-FISH (*Diodon*); body, round, and covered with spines. By taking air into its capacious stomach, this fish can inflate itself spherically; and thus, erecting its spines, defend itself when in danger. They are found in the seas of hot countries, and attain the size of one or two feet.

i. The GLOBE-FISH (*Tetraodon*); the belly so large that it projects beyond the mouth; the head is short, and when the fish is inflated, it appears to be all belly. It lives in the Mediterranean and East-Indian Seas.

Plate 12.

a. The Short Sun-fish (*Orthagoriscus mola*) looks as if cut off behind, and bound with a ribbon. When full grown, it weighs several hundred pounds, and is said to shine in the night. It is found in the Mediterranean Sea and the Atlantic Ocean.

b. The Great Pipe-fish (*Syngnathus acus*); head, with a long snout, at the end of which lies the small, toothless mouth. The development of the young is very curious. The male receives the eggs in sacs, formed by the swelling of the skin of his belly. The young are hatched in these pockets, which open and let them out.

c. The Sea-horse (*Hippocampus*); belly, seven-edged; tail, prehensile; in head and neck resembling a horse; length, from three to six inches. When alive, the Sea-horse is straight; in death, it crooks itself like the letter S. It is found in the Mediterranean.

d. The Sea-dragon (*Pegasus draco*) differs from the Sea-horse in the snout projecting far over the mouth; the breast-fins, wing-like; and the belly-fins, like simple threads. This fish is about one and a half feet long, and is found in the East-Indian Seas.

BONY FISHES.

A. Apodes. — These fishes are soft-finned, without ventrals.

e. Electric Eel (*Gymnotus electricus*); body, elongated and covered with thick, soft skin; the back fin reaches to the point of the tail; the upper jaw projects over the under; the color is reddish; the length, from four to six feet. This curious fish is found in the ponds and rivers of South America. It imparts such powerful electric shocks, that horses which are driven into the water, and men who attempt to seize it, are often prostrated by it.

f. The Common EEL (*Anguilla acutirostris*); body, cylindrical, nearly naked, furnished with breast and back fins; the scales are small, and quite imbedded in the slimy skin; color, dark-green, lighter on the sides, and silvery or yellowish on the belly. The usual length is from one to three feet; but there are also larger ones. It is found in most European rivers. It feeds on insects, worms, and fish roes. The Eel is tenacious of life; its flesh is savory, but hard to digest.

g. The Conger EEL (*Gymnothorax* (*Murœna*) *Helena*) has only one spinal fin, and mottled brown and yellow. This fish is found in the Mediterranean Sea, grows to three or more feet, and is exceedingly voracious. Its flesh is very savory, and was highly prized by the Romans.

h. SEA-WOLF, SEA-CAT, SWINE-FISH (*Anarrhichas lupus*); body, smooth and slimy; mouth, large, and armed with many teeth. It feeds on crabs and shell-fish; is from five to seven feet long, and inhabits the Atlantic. Its flesh is eaten fresh, dried, or salted; and the Icelanders make use of its skin for shoes.

i. SWORD-FISH (*Xiphias gladius*); back, violet-color; belly and sides, white; body, spindle-shaped, with scales almost invisible. The mouth is toothless, but very rough. The upper jaw terminates in a very long, flat, sharp sword, with which it cuts down the sea-plants upon which it feeds. This fish lives in the Mediterranean Sea, and sometimes comes into the Baltic; it is twenty feet long, and weighs from four to five hundred pounds. Its flesh is pleasant to the taste; and the fins, which are salted, are regarded as delicacies.

Plate 13.

B. Jugulares. — These fishes have fins on the throat or neck.

a. The Star-gazer (*Uranoscopus scaber*); head, flat and warty; the eyes appear to be looking to the sky; mouth, cut vertically. This fish is armed with two pairs of retractile spines; it is never more than fourteen inches long; is edible, and found chiefly in the Mediterranean.

b. The Common Hake (*Gadus* (*Merlucius*) *vulgaris*) has two dorsal fins. The Hake is from twenty to thirty inches long; is of a reddish-brown color; is generally caught with the hook at night, salted and dried.

c. The Common Ling (*G.* (*Lota*) *molva, barbatus*), is rather long; has a projecting upper jaw and a barbel. It is peculiar to Norway, and used as the stockfish.

d. The Cod (*G.* (*Morrhua*) *vulgaris*) has three dorsal fins; and on the mouth a barbel. It is from two to three feet long, and weighs fourteen to thirty pounds, and sometimes more. The Cod is found between forty and seventy-five degrees north latitude. It is olive-green above, and whitish beneath, with yellowish spots on the sides. Some twenty thousand men are employed in the cod-fisheries off the American coast; and, although millions are caught yearly, their number is undiminished, inasmuch as one female has from four to eight million eggs. The Cod is usually salted, and is an important article of commerce.

e. HADDOCK (*G.* (*Morrhua*) *æglefinus*) is also a valuable fish; brown above, and silvery-white below.

f. The DORSE (*G. gallarias*); head and back, brown; sides, silvery, lined and spotted. The Dorse is found in the Baltic and North Seas, and is much sought, on account of its savory flesh.

g. The POOR, or POWER, COD (*G. minutus*) is scarcely eight inches long, and of a yellowish-brown color.

h. The BURBOT, or EELPOUT (*G. lota*), has two dorsal fins, and jaws of equal length. The body is black, mottled with yellow, and covered with slime. The head is large and flat. The Burbot is the only species of this family which lives in fresh water. It is from two to three feet long, and weighs from ten to twelve pounds; its flesh is savory; liver, highly valued.

PLATE 14.

a. The viviparous BLENNY (*Blennius viviparus*) is about six inches in length; nostrils, tube-like; covered with a slimy mucus. The Blenny inhabits the North and Baltic Seas. Its flesh is of little value. In the female, there are often found three hundred young ones.

C. THORACICI. — These fishes have the ventrals on the breast, directly under the pectorals.

b. The Black GOBY, or ROCKFISH (*Gobius niger*), is yellowish, with blackish-brown spots; rather small; it lives at the bottom of the sea, and feeds on worms. Its flesh is savory; it spawns at the mouth of rivers.

c. The Sucking Fish (*Echeneïs remora*); caudal fin pointed; the back, black; sides, lighter; head covered with singularly formed plates, which can slide forward and back, and by means of which they attach themselves to vessels and sharks. They are found in the Mediterranean and Atlantic Ocean; they measure from one to two feet, and are not good for food.

d. The Dragon's Head (*Scorpæna*) has a spiny head; the back has only one fin; the ventral is broad, and under it is an oval fin; around the head is a pointed collar, which gives it a very peculiar appearance. It is found in the Mediterranean and North Seas, and is over three feet long; its flesh, which is lean and tough, is eaten by the Italians.

e. The Mackerel (*Scomber scombrus*) has small fins on each side of the tail; the back is blue, with small, black lines; upper parts, silvery. It is from twelve to twenty-four inches long, and weighs from one to three pounds. Mackerel are found in shoals, on the Atlantic coasts. The flesh is savory, and is eaten both fresh and salted. The mackerel-fishery is an important branch of commerce. It is a voracious fish, and dangerous to herrings.

f. The Tunny (*Scomber* (*Thynnus*) *vulgaris*) has from eight to ten fins on its tail; the back is steel-blue, sides silvery, and the pectorals yellowish. It is generally from one to two feet long; occasionally twelve to eighteen feet, and sometimes weighs five hundred pounds. The Tunny is widely diffused, and very voracious. The time of spawning is in May and June, when they move to the shores in immense shoals. The Tunny is an important fish to the Sicilians, who employ large nets, divided into compartments, in their fishery. Its flesh is red and nutritious, and eaten salted and fresh.

g. The STICKLE-BACK (*Gasterosteus*) has one dorsal fin, with three spines before it; the body is of metallic brilliancy, being covered with silvery scales as far as the tail. In place of the ventral, it has a single spine, which affords it protection from voracious fish in the rivers, where it abounds. It is caught for oil, and for food for ducks and pigs. It builds a nest for its young.

h. The Climbing PERCH (*Anabas scandens*) has a long, broad head; it is found in the East Indies, and climbs bushes and trees, by means of the anal spines.

i. The River BULL-HEAD, or MILLER'S THUMB (*Cottus gobio*), has a very thick head, slimy and warty body; color, brown above, and white below; it has two dorsals and one ventral fin. The Bull-head is found in brooks, and is seldom more than seven inches long. It swims rapidly, and its flesh is savory and healthy.

GURNARDS (*Trigla*). — Spine-rayed fishes, which have the head variously mailed.

k. The Grey GURNARD (*Trigla gurnardus*); the head enclosed in a bony mail; two dorsal fins. It inhabits the North Sea, and feeds upon mussels, and is used for food.

l. The Flying GURNARD (*T. volitans*) has beautiful green pectorals, spotted with blue; the body is violet above, and silvery beneath. These Gurnards are found in shoals, in the seas of hot countries, but are rarely seen in European seas; they fly out of the sea when pursued by voracious fishes.

Plate 15.

a. The DORY, or DORÉE (*Zeus faber*); body, flat; its first dorsal has projecting, bony spines; on each side of its gold-colored body is a gray spot; back, dark; mouth, furnished with small teeth. The Dory is found in the Mediterranean and North Seas; its flesh, particularly that of the larger kind, is savory. It measures from one to one and a third feet.

b. The SOLE (*Pleuronectes (Solea) vulgaris*); the only vertebrate whose body is not symmetrically formed. The eyes lie mostly above, on the right side, and the whole body is flat and compressed, so that when the mouth of the fish is turned toward the observer, the dorsal terminates one side, and the anal the other; the anus lies near the head. Its color is grayish-brown, spotted with orange. There are many varieties of Soles; their flesh is excellent, and it is eaten fresh and dried.

c. The HALIBUT (*P. (Hippoglossus) vulgaris*). The body is smooth; ash-gray on one side, and white on the other; the side lines strongly curved over the pectorals. It is from three to six feet long, and often weighs several hundred pounds.

d. The Common PERCH (*Perca fluviatilis*); scales, rough; head, naked; glossy yellow-green, with black cross-stripes; lower fins, red. The Perch is common in lakes and rivers. It weighs from two to four pounds; is exceedingly voracious, not sparing even its own kind. The flesh is savory and healthy.

e. The Pike PERCH (*Perca lucioperca*) is green, with brown cross-stripes.

f. The RUFFE, or POPE (*Acerina cernua*); head, thick; color of the back, green, with black points; sides, yellowish; belly, white. It is from six to eight inches long; is much esteemed for food.

g. The Plain MULLET (*Mullus surmuletus, et barbatus*) has long barbels on the lower jaw; head, somewhat depressed; color, a beautiful pink, with golden stripes. This fish is most abundant in the Mediterranean, though inhabiting the fresh waters and coasts of temperate and tropical regions. Its flesh is savory, and it was highly valued by the ancient Romans.

h. Rainbow WRASSE (*Labrus (Julis) vulgaris*) is from three to four inches in length; lips, thick and movable; color above is blue with orange stripes. It is found in the Mediterranean Sea, and sometimes attaches itself to the feet of bathers.

D. ABDOMINALES. — These fishes have ventrals behind the pectorals, like feet.

i. The Gray MULLET (*Mugil cephalus*), is covered with large scales, or plates. This fish is one foot long. It is found on our coasts.

PLATE 16.

a. The LOACH (*Cobitis barbatula*) has six barbels about the mouth; the head is smooth; body, cylindrical and gray, marbled with white. The Loach attains the length of from three to four inches, and is found in clear streams with gravelled bottom. Its flesh is tender and agreeable.

b. The Ground LOACH (*C. fossilis*) has ten barbels around the mouth; its body is black, with long yellow stripes; the belly is orange-color, with black spots. It attains a length of ten to twelve inches, lives in the slime of rivers and ponds, which it disturbs when the weather changes; for which reason it is sometimes kept in glasses, with sand and water, to foretell the weather.

c. The Spined LOACH (*C. tænia*) has a forked-like spine under the eye; it has an elongated row of black spots on its yellowish sides. It attains the length of five inches; its flesh is tough.

d. The SHEAT-FISH (*Silurus*) has two long barbels above the mouth, and four short ones below; the head, compressed, frog-like; the back is round, and greenish-black; belly, pale-green; and the whole spotted with black. It attains the length of six feet, and weighs about one hundred pounds. The flesh is white, flat, and sweetish. It is very voracious.

e. The Common FLYING-FISH (*Exocœtus volitans*). The pectorals of this fish are about as long as its body. They are found in warm and temperate seas; the species vary from three to twelve inches in length. They can sustain themselves in the air for a few moments; their flesh is savory, but dry.

f. The HERRING (*Clupea harengus*). Its head is small; the lower jaw protrudes beyond the upper; the body is much compressed; silvery, with a blackish back. It is about ten inches long. The Herring inhabits the northern seas. Whole fleets of vessels go out to catch Herrings. Thousands of millions are taken in a year, and perhaps as many more fall a prey to voracious fish. They are smoked and salted. The Dutch understand best this preparation; and, on that account, the Dutch Herrings are much esteemed.

g. The Anchovy (*C. (Engraulis) encrasicolus*). Its upper jaw is protruding; the body is slender and silvery, about a span in length. It is a native of the North and Mediterranean Seas, where it is caught in immense numbers for exportation.

Cyprinidæ, or Carp Family. — There are many species in this family, of which we describe the following: —

h. The Common Carp (*Cyprinus carpio*); mouth, toothless, ornamented with four barbels; the body is covered with large striped scales; the back, dark-green; the sides, yellowish; and the belly, white. The Carp originated in Southern Europe, and was carried to England in 1514, and to Denmark in 1560; the farther north they go, the smaller they are. The river Carps are better than the pond Carps; but the best are those which are kept in ponds through which a river flows. Carps are tenacious of life, and attain the weight of forty pounds.

i. The Tench (*C. (Tinca) vulgaris*); barbels, very short; fins, very thick and opaque; the body, slender, and covered with small scales. Its colors are various: above, dark; beneath, changing to yellow; fins, dark-violet. The Tench lives in still waters, and attains a weight of from seven to eight pounds. Its flesh is tender, and agreeable to the taste.

Plate 17.

a. The Bream (*C. brama*) grows broad and thick, weighs from twelve to twenty pounds, and is three feet long. Its scales are large; back, dark-green; sides, silvery; caudal, yellow. It is found mostly in northern waters.

b. The ORF (*C. orphus*) is orange-red, with silvery belly. It is bred as an ornament, the flesh being valueless.

c. The German CARP (*C. carassius*) is very broad, and but a span long, without barbels, and agreeable to the taste.

d. The Red EYE (*C. erythrophthalmus*) has red fins, and yellowish-red rings about its eyes.

e. The ROACH (*C. (Leuciscus) rutilus*) has also red fins and red rings about the eyes.

f. The IDE (*C. (Leuciscus) idus*) has a stout body, with red ventral and anal fins.

g. The CHUB (*C. (L.) Jeses*) has a thick, stubbed head, bordered with blue; scales, violet-color. Its flesh is savory.

h. The Dobule ROACH (*C. (L.) dobula*); above, dark olive-green; belly, white; pectorals, yellowish; ventrals and anal, red.

PLATE 18.

a. The DACE, DARE, DART (*C. (Leuciscus) vulgaris*); body, elongated; fins, grayish; very common in the south of Germany.

b. The Nosed CARP (*C. nasus*) is a slender fish; upper jaw protruding; color, bluish; fins, red; common in fresh water.

c. The MINNOW (*C. (Leuciscus) phoxinus*); body, cylindrical; color, variegated; gills, yellow; back, dark-blue; abdomen, silvery. These beautiful little fish are very savory.

d. The Prussian Carp (*C. vimba*); the upper jaw projecting over the lower one. It is one foot long.

e. The Gray Carp (*C. amarus*). These are the smallest of all Carps, being but two inches long, and half an inch broad. They are greenish-yellow above, and silvery below. They are bitter to the taste; inhabit running water.

f. The Gudgeon (*C. (Gobio) fluviatilis*) has a slim body, is six inches long; fins, reddish; dorsals and caudal spotted with black. It is found in rivers and ponds with sandy bottoms, and is savory to the taste.

g. The Barbel (*C. (Barbus) vulgaris*). Its mouth has four barbels; upper jaw protruding; in body resembling the Pike; back, olive-colored; sides, whitish, with a greenish tint; fins, reddish. The Barbel prefers running waters and animal food. It weighs from six to fifteen pounds, and is esteemed for food.

h. The White Bream (*C. blicca*); pectorals and ventrals, red; body, broad. It is widely diffused.

i. The Gold-fish (*C. auratus*) is indigenous to China and Japan, where it is found of most beautiful colors. It is kept with us in garden-ponds and glasses.

k. The Salmon (*Salmo salar*) has a slightly protruding upper jaw. Its mouth is armed with teeth; back, black; sides, bluish; abdomen, silvery. Almost all Salmons are spotted. The male has, on the lower jaw, a cartilaginous hook, bent upwards. Salmons inhabit the northern seas, whence they visit the rivers of both continents in large numbers to spawn; they go in regular order, the females in advance. They winter in the seas, and return to the same rivers every year. They live on small fish and worms, and weigh from twenty-five to fifty pounds, and more. Their flesh is excellent, and is prepared in many ways.

l. The Common, or River, TROUT (*S. fario*) is from six to twenty inches long, and of different colors; the colder the water, the darker the color. Its sides are yellow; it is spotted with red. The Trout swims with great rapidity; it feeds on small fishes and insects, and spawns in the fall. Its flesh is considered finer than that of any other fish.

PLATE 19.

a. The Salmon TROUT (*S. trutta*) is dark-gray, with spots on the back and sides. It weighs from eight to ten pounds.

b. The HUCHEN (*S. hucho*); back, sides, and fins (except the pectorals), with brown spots. Its head is more pointed than in the Salmon Trout. It attains the length of from three to five feet; is peculiar to the Danube, and its southern tributaries, and has very savory flesh.

c. The Lake TROUT (*S. lacustris*); back, dark; sides, light-blue; lower parts, silvery, with small, half-moon-like spots. Its flesh is yellowish, and much esteemed; it attains a weight of fifty pounds.

d. The CHAR (*S. salvelinus*); its back is brown, with orange-colored spots, bordered with white on the sides; pectorals and ventrals, red. Its flesh is valued.

e. The GRAYLING (*S. (Thymallus) vulgaris*); dorsals, violet; below, spotted greenish-brown. Its back is striped with black. It is found in cold waters, and is very savory.

f. The Gwyniad (*S. Wartmanni*) is blue above; silvery below; body, long, and without spots. It inhabits the lakes of Southern Germany, where it is found in great numbers, and is to the inhabitants what the Herring is to those of more northern climes. They are caught only when three years old, and are eaten fresh or pickled. They are an important article of export. Their flesh is excellent, and easy of digestion.

g. The Smelt (*S. (Osmerus) eperlanus*) is greenish above, and silvery beneath. It is a small fish, living in the sea, and at the mouth of rivers; flesh, excellent.

h. The Pike (*Esox lucius*) has an oblong snout, broad and depressed. Its color varies; back, blackish-green; sides, gray, spotted with yellow, and the abdomen white, dotted with black; the yearlings are all green. They grow rapidly; are from eighteen to twenty inches long in their first year; and, when fully grown, they measure from six to eight feet, and weigh about forty pounds. The whole mouth is armed with teeth. The Pike is very voracious. It not only eats fish, but also birds, frogs, &c. It is found in the fresh waters of both continents.

i. The Garpike (*E. belone*) has the head and body greatly elongated; jaws studded with numerous small teeth; bones, green. It is found in all seas, and caught by thousands in the Mediterranean.

Plate 20.

Cirripeds (a subdivision of the *Crustacea*, the chief division of which is represented on Plate 27) are placed here on account of their resemblance to the Shells. This singular order of animals comes between the Articulates and the Mollusca. They have no head, but a horny upper lip, on each side of which are articulated feelers, two pairs of toothed jaws, and a membranous lower lip, and along the articulated body ten to twelve pairs of tufty arms. Their lime shell is generally composed of several pieces united together. They are attached to rocks or other objects by the base of their shells, or by a membranous peduncle. To this class belong the following: —

a. The BALANUS, or Acorn-shell BARNACLE (*Balanus tintinnabulum*) has six tulip-like standing shell-leaves fixed upon a lower shell, striated crosswise. The animal comes out from the opening above, and below it is attached to vessels and rocks. The most beautiful of these are found in the East Indies.

b. 1 and 2. Another BARNACLE (*Coronula balænaris*) is similar to the preceding, only the inner compartments are like those of a poppy-head. It attaches itself to the skin of whales.

c. The Sea TULIP (*Lepas anatifera*) has a tough stalk or peduncle by which it fixes itself, and often in great numbers, to the bottom of the sea, and to ships. It has two large, broad valves, and one smaller and narrower.

MOLLUSCA, OR MOLLUSKS. — These are animals which have a soft body enveloped in a muscular skin, and mostly protected by a shell. They have a distinct nervous system, a heart with arteries and veins, and perfect organs for the digestion of food, respiration, and reproduction. The body of most of the Mollusks is a shapeless, soft mass; half of them are deprived of a head, and organs of sense. A few of them have organs of locomotion. Their movements are slow. The body is covered with a contractile and slimy membrane, which envelops the animal like a mantle. A calcareous shell, with one or two valves, forms the exterior envelope of the animal. The circulation of the blood is complete. The heart is simple or double, or there are three ventricles. The blood is white and cold. The Mollusks breathe either water through branchiæ, or air by means of lungs or air sacs. The sexes are separate, or united in the same animal.

Mollusks are spread over the whole earth, and live generally in the sea; some, however, live in rivers and ponds, and others upon land.

ACEPHALA have no head, breathe through branchiæ, and are enclosed in a bivalve shell; have a mouth opening on one end, and another opening on the other end. They have a large liver; and, toward the back, a heart with two ventricles. The posterior opening serves for respiration; and, in some species, gives issue to two tubes, through which water goes in and out. The fleshy fore part of the animal is prolonged, in many of these animals, into a kind of bent foot, by means of which they move forward, and attach themselves.

d. The Giant MUSSEL, or CLAM (*Tridacna gigas*), has furrows and tile-like scales. These shells sometimes grow to the weight of six hundred pounds, and are used in several of the churches of Paris as *bénitiers*.

e. The SCALLOP (*Pecten gigas*, or *maximus*).

f. The TEREBRATULA (*Terebratula*). Its shells are unequal; the larger one has a protruding hook, pierced by a hole, through which passes a muscle with which the shell attaches itself to other shells.

g. The OYSTER (*Ostrea edulis*); shells, irregular and toothless. They are attached to rocks in the sea; valued as an article of food.

h. The Thorny OYSTER (*Spondylus radula*); shells, spiny or rough, with two strong teeth.

i. The Pearl MUSSEL (*Mytilus (Avicula) margaritifera*); shells, semi-circular, toothless. The splendid mother-of-pearl is on the inner side of the shell. It measures about eight inches in diameter. These shells are found in the Indian and Persian seas, and furnish the real oriental pearls. Some divers let themselves down into the water, at the risk of their lives, to obtain these valuable shells.

PLATE 21.

a. The Ark MUSSEL (*Arca Noæ*); shells, elongated, nearly four-edged; the hinge forms a straight line armed with small teeth. This shell resembles a vessel.

b. The PINNA (*Pinna*) is conical; it stands with its pointed part in the sand. From the upper part of this mussel protrudes a silk-like tuft, of which the Italians make stockings and gloves.

c. The Common Sea MUSSEL (*Mytilus edulis*); the fore part, pointed; the hind part, broader. It is found in all seas.

d. The River MUSSEL (*Anodonta cygnæa*) is found in ponds.

e. The PAINTER'S MUSSEL (*Mya pictorum*) has a strong tooth on the hinge of the shell. It is used for the preservation of colors.

f. The Cockle-shell (*Cardium*) has four strong teeth in each shell. There are many beautiful varieties in all seas.

g. The Horny-heart Mussel (*Cyclas cornea*) is found in the slime of ditches.

h. The Sauce Mussel (*Tellina*); shells, flat, red and white; or yellow and white.

i. The Venus Mussel (*Venus*); shells, round or oval; hinge, toothed.

k. The Razor-shell (*Solen*) resembles a razor-sheath; is gaping at both ends.

l. The Piddock (*Pholas*). Beside its principal shells, which are gaping, it has other smaller shells; it digs into mud and rocks, and is eaten.

m. The Boring, or Ship, Worm (*Teredo navalis*); shell, exceedingly hard, and armed with rasp-like imbrications. They burrow into almost any substance, and have caused much damage to ships and piers. They are from six to twelve inches long, and thick as the finger. They originated in the Indies, and have been carried by ships into other countries. Vessels are coppered to protect them against this animal.

Plate 22.

Gasteropods, or Univalves. — These have a distinct head, provided with feelers; and small eyes. On the belly is a muscular expansion which enables them to crawl; they are partly naked, or enveloped in a calcareous shell. Those which live in the sea, breathe by means of branchiæ; those on land, by means of lungs, or air sacs. The sexes are separate or united.

a. The Skittle, or Cone, SHELL (*Conus*); shell, conical; opening, elongated, narrow, and without teeth. Some of them are beautifully colored, and amateurs pay a great price for them.

b. The Tiger SHELL (*Cypræa*); shell, smooth; opening, small and narrow.

c. The COWRIE (*C. moneta*) is not only used to ornament the harness of asses and horses, but as money in Africa and the East Indies; a very inconvenient kind of money, as it requires about a thousand to make a dollar.

d. The Mitre SHELL (*Mitra*). The shell runs to a point; it has orange-colored spots on a white ground. The flesh of this animal is poisonous; it is capable of making a severe wound with its tongue. It inhabits the East-Indian seas.

e. The Roller SHELL (*Voluta Æthiopica*) is very large and edible; color of the shell, a reddish-brown. It is used as a vase in the East Indies.

f. The Wing SHELL (*Strombus auris Dianæ*).

g. The Armed Wing SHELL (*S. pugilis*). This animal is called "the fighter," because of the continual motion which it makes with the point of its foot, striking here and there.

h. The Purple SHELL (*Murex*); shell, rough and spiny; generally brown or grayish-white. The ancients prepared their purple color from a liquor furnished by this animal.

i. The Trumpet SHELL (*Tritonium tuba*); shell, smooth, spotted with brown, and toothed at the opening. If one breaks the point and blows into it, it produces a trumpet-like sound. The shell is a foot long; its flesh is good to eat.

k. The Helmet SHELL (*Cassis*) is similar to the Tiger Shell.

l. The Harp SHELL (*Harpa*) is found in the seas of the East and West Indies; shell, broad and ventricose; opening, very wide above; spirals ornamented with projecting ridges.

m. The Tun SHELL (*Dolium*) is thin and ventricose, with roundish hoops.

n. The Hoop SHELL (*Trochus*); the spirals very large below, and pointed above.

o. The Top SHELL (*Turbo*); shell with a round opening.

p. The COCKLE-STAIRS (*Scalaria communis*) has a white shell, with many spirals; the opening is round. This species is frequently found in the Mediterranean.

q. The East-India COCKLE-SHELL (*S. pretiosa*). The spirals of this shell are much farther apart, and this Cockle is much rarer than the preceding.

r. The Common Water SNAIL (*Nerita*); shell, hemispherical; opening, large, and shaped like a crescent. It is found in seas and rivers.

s. The Chrysalis SHELL (*Pupa uva*) has a long, broad, striped shell, with a round mouth.

Land-Snail Family — *Helicidæ.* — These are distributed over the whole world; there are some four thousand living species, and several hundred fossil.

t. The Roman SNAIL (*Helix pomatia*) has a yellowish-gray or grayish-white shell. They shut themselves within their shells in winter. Europeans eat this species of snail.

Plate 23.

a. The Common Tree Snail (*Helix nemoralis*) is well known; shell, yellow or red, with brown bands.

b. The Glutton Snail (*Bulimus decollatus*) is oblong; the point looks as if broken off.

c. The Pond Snail (*Limnæa stagnalis*); shell, thin, spiral, pointed; mouth, large. This Snail is found everywhere in stagnant waters.

d. The Disk Snail (*Planorbis vortex*); wound round, like a cornet.

e. The Ear Shell (*Haliotis Iris*); shell shaped like an ear, pierced with many holes. It is remarkable for the beauty of its pearl, which glitters with all the colors of the rainbow.

f. The Rock Limpet (*Patella*); shell in the form of a ladle; common to all seas; found creeping on or adhering to rocks.

g. The Male Limpet (*Chiton*); shell, oval, hollow, similar to the articulated body of a beetle.

NAKED SNAILS, WITHOUT SHELLS.

h. The Slug (*Limax*) is noted for an abundant secretion of mucus; the mouth has a horny upper jaw, with which this animal gnaws plants and fruits, and makes great havoc in our gardens.

i. The Sea Hare (*Aplysia*). Its head is adorned with four tentacles, the two longest of which are in the form of ears.

The Pteropoda, or Pteropods; mollusks, which

inhabit the open sea, where they move in immense numbers together.

k. The WHALE-FOOD (*Clio borealis*) is furnished with two fin-like appendages. They inhabit the Arctic seas; move in swarms, and form the principal food of Right Whales.

CEPHALOPODS, OR CUTTLE-FISH. — They have a distinct head, with two large eyes; the mouth, in the middle of the head; long tentacles, which serve for feet and arms, armed with suckers, and with which they walk or seize hold of their prey. Many of these animals have a sac, which secretes a very dark liquid, called ink, which they use to color the water when they wish to conceal themselves. This liquid is known by painters under the name of sepia, or Indian ink. These animals are voracious and powerful.

l. a. and *b.* The NAUTILUS (*Nautilus*) lives in a beautiful shell, containing many chambers. This animal has twenty pairs of arms, and is found in the Indian seas.

m. The ARGONAUT, or PAPER-SAILOR (*Argonauta*). The female sits entirely free, in a thin shell, holding herself firm by her arms. The male is much smaller, and has neither shell, nor fin-like extended arms. The shell of the Argonaut is formed and repaired by a secretion contained in the glands of the arms.

n. The CUTTLE-FISH (*Sepia*) has ten arms, two of which are very long. The body is contained in a bordered sac, which encloses the cuttle-bone. They are from six inches to three feet in length.

INSECTS.

PLATE 24.

INSECTS. — The body is generally enveloped in a hard skin; sometimes by a soft one. It is composed of three distinct parts, — the head, chest or thorax, and hind body or abdomen. The head has either single or compound eyes, and antennæ, or feelers, which are, doubtless, connected with the sense of hearing. The mouth has an upper and lower lip; two upper and two lower jaws, and a tongue. The thorax is composed of three pieces, to which the legs and wings are attached; the abdomen is articulated. The organs of respiration lie on each side of the body. The heart consists of a long tube, under the covering of the back, and has small holes for the admission of the yellow or colorless blood, and valves within to prevent its escaping.

The nervous system is composed of an articulated cord, under the digestive tube, from which the nerves go to the various parts of the body. The sexes are separate; the females are either viviparous or oviparous. Some lay few, others many, eggs; for example, the wasp lays twenty thousand; the queen bee, from forty to fifty thousand eggs.

The metamorphoses, or transformations, of insects

are wonderful; the same insect, at different ages, may easily be mistaken for as many different animals. Only a small number of insects emerge from the egg in a perfect form. Others appear in their first state like a worm; they are then called larvæ. Larvæ of butterflies are called caterpillars, and are provided with feet. The larva period is that of infancy, and much the longest. When fully grown, the larva encloses itself in some peculiar cell, as in a shroud; and it is then called a pupa, or chrysalis. After a time, the insect comes out of its cell in a perfect state, to enjoy a new life, and is then called the imago. The ancients regarded this metamorphosis as the symbol of immortality. The industry of insects is very remarkable. They are divided into —

I. COLEOPTERA, OR SHEATH-WINGED INSECTS. — The Sheath-winged Insects are armed with jaws. They have six legs and four wings, the two upper of which are horny covers; and the two under ones are membranous, and lie folded under the others, when the insect is in a state of repose. They undergo a perfect metamorphosis. The larva feeds on animal and vegetable substances, like the perfect Beetle. The pupa is immovable and shows all the parts of a perfect insect.

a. The Rhinoceros BEETLE (*Oryctes nasicornis*) is of a chestnut-brown color, with a horn on the helmet of the head, bent backward. This Beetle is found about the North-Sea coast and vicinity.

b. The Dung BEETLE (*Scarabæus stercorarius*) is blue-black; found chiefly on horse-dung.

c. The Horn Dung BEETLE (*Cobris lunaris*) is found mostly on cow-dung; is a very handsome Beetle, and has a tolerably large horn on its crescent-shaped helmet;

it is nearly as large as the Dung Beetle, and of a glossy black color.

d. The Pill-chafer (*Ateuchus sacer*) has a six-pointed helmet.

e. The Lesser Dung Beetle (*Aphodius*) is egg-shaped, about the size of an apple-seed; it is black, with red wing-covers.

f. The Cockchafer (*Melolontha vulgaris*). The larva of this Beetle lives four years in the ground, gnawing the roots of trees and plants, then becomes a pupa, and in its fifth year comes out a perfect Cockchafer.

g. The Great Cockchafer (*M. fullo*) has beautiful wings, mottled brown and white. It eats the tops of poplars and oaks; it is seldom caught on account of its rapid flight.

h. The Rose-chafer (*Cetonia aurea*) is of a brilliant greenish gold-color; lives as a grub in ant-heaps, and is particularly injurious to roses.

i. The Stag Beetle (*Lucanus cervus*); a most beautiful dark-brown, or blackish, Chafer. The male has stag-like horns (large protruding upper jaws) with which it can pinch hard.

j. The Bark Beetle (*Bostrichus typographus*), with pointed wing-covers and wedge-like feelers, is less than a grain of wheat, but does a great deal of harm to trees in its larva state.

k. The Grave-digger (*Necrophorus vespillo*) is a remarkable Chafer. It buries dead animals, as for example, mice, or moles; and the female lays her eggs in the flesh of the buried animal. These eggs produce beautifully variegated grubs, which become Chafers in six weeks.

l. The Goldsmith, or Gardener, BEETLE (*Carabus auratus*) has beautiful gold-green wing-covers. It is useful in destroying great quantities of worms and insects.

All the Beetles above described have either leafy or button-like feelers.

m. The SYCOPHANT (*Calosama inquisitor*) is of a copper-brown color; wing-covers, spotted and lined. It kills injurious insects, particularly caterpillars, and is not very numerous.

n. The Sand SPARKLER (*Cicindela*) is almost everywhere in sandy places. It runs quickly and flies rapidly.

o. The Flour BEETLE (*Tenebrio molitor*) is long and of a dark color; in the larva state it is called the meal-worm.

p. The Water BEETLE (*Hydrophilus*) is dark-brown; antennæ, wedge-like.

q. The Leaping BEETLE (*Elater*). If placed upon its back, it springs into the air in order to come down on its feet.

r. The Green WEEVIL (*Curculio chlorophanus*) has a long trunk.

s. The DEATH-WATCH (*Anobium*). This insect and another kind gnaw into books and wood-work when in a larva state. The Death-watch produces a sound resembling the ticking of a watch.

t. The FIREFLY (*Lampyris splendidula*). The end of the abdomen is soft, smooth, and shining in the night. Not only the male, but the female gives a light. The latter and the larva have no wings.

u. The Spanish FLY (*Lytta vesicatoria*) is green, and of metallic brilliancy; body, elongated. It contains an irritating matter, which is used for blisters.

v. The MAY-WORM (*Meloë proscarabæus*) is dark-blue,

of metallic brilliancy; wing-covers, short and soft; antennæ, round and articulated.

w. The Carpenter BEETLE (*Lamia ædilis*) is gray; the antennæ, three times as long as the body.

x. The Great Goat BEETLE (*Prionus coriaceus*); dark chestnut-brown; three points on its horny collar; antennæ serrated like a saw; found in leafy woods.

y. The Lily CHAFER (*Lema*) is scarlet-red; head, black; found between the leaves of lilies, lily of the valley, and iris; it makes a piping noise when taken in the hand.

z. The LADY BIRD (*Coccinella septempunctata*); roundish, with seven black points upon the red wing-covers; its larva destroys a great many injurious Plant Lice, or Aphides.

II. ORTHOPTERA, OR STRAIGHT-WINGED INSECTS. — They have six legs, are armed with jaws, and have soft, membranous, and veined wing-covers; lower wings, straight and crosswise. Their transformation is imperfect, as the wings are wanting in the young, and grow by degrees.

a. The EARWIG (*Forficula*); feet with three tarsi; a pair of nippers at the tail; it lives, generally, in the bark of trees and old wood-work. The female covers and protects the eggs and tender young ones.

b. The COCKROACH (*Blatta*); brown; wing-covers, long; head concealed beneath the shield of the thorax. These insects are well known as being very voracious; they eat, not only meal, bread, and other articles of food, but leather and cloth.

c. The MANTIS (*Mantis religiosa*) is similar to the House Cricket, but carries its head, with its large eyes, upright. These carnivorous insects eat each other and other insects.

d. The Green Locust (*Locusta viridissima*) is green, with very long antennæ; the female has a long, sword-like appendage. This Locust makes immense springs, with its long legs.

e. The Mole Cricket (*Gryllotalpa vulgaris*). Its fore feet are large and like hands; hind feet, short. It digs subterranean passages with its fore feet, like the Moles, and does much injury to fields, where they are found in great numbers, by cutting off the roots of plants.

f. The House Cricket (*Gryllus domesticus*); pale-yellow; head, round, and provided with long antennæ. It inhabits human habitations, and seeks places where it is warm; its sharp and monotonous tones are heard at night, when it goes in quest of food.

g. The Field Cricket (*G. campestris*) is dark-brown; in warm weather, it chirps the whole day in front of the hole it has dug in the earth.

h. The Migratory Locust (*Acridium migratorium*); wing-covers, gray or brown, speckled with black; under wings, green and unspotted. This Locust inhabits Asia and Africa, and is rarely found in Europe. They are a scourge, appearing from time to time in such swarms as to darken the air, eating up whole fields of grain where they settle.

i. The Rattle Cricket (*A. stridulum*); back and wings, red, bordered with black. They appear at the end of summer, in the outskirts of forests.

III. Neuroptera, or Nerve-Winged Insects. — They have six legs, are armed with jaws, and have four naked, membranous wings; some of them undergo a perfect, others an imperfect, transformation. Most of them live, at first, in the water; when winged, they live on the land.

j. The WATER-LADY (*Libellula*); the abdomen elongated, and ending in small pincers; its beautifully colored wings are large, brilliant, and glossy. It feeds on insects caught in flight, and flies rapidly. Called, also, Darning Needles, Mosquito Hawks, and Dragon Flies.

k. The MAY FLY (*Ephemera*); antennæ, with three articulations; abdomen terminating in two or three bristle-like appendages. The larva lives for years in mud or water, and comes out by millions as winged insects, which live only a few hours.

l. The DRAGON-FLY, or CADDIS-FLY (*Phryganea*). Many species of this Fly are found, in their imperfect state, in lakes and ponds. It bears much resemblance to a Butterfly; its transformation is complete.

m. The Pearl FLY (*Hemerobius perla*); green and beautiful to the eye, but of disagreeable odor. Its larva feeds on the Aphis, or Plant Louse.

n. The Ant LION (*Myrmecoleon*) is similar to the Water-lady, but not so quick in its motions; it undergoes a perfect metamorphosis. The larva, known as the Ant Lion, is a cunning capturer of ants. It digs a conical pit in fine sand, and when an ant comes to the edge of it, the sand gives way and the ant falls in; if it tries to crawl out, the Ant Lion sprinkles sand upon it until it falls to the bottom, where the larva seizes it with its strong pincers and sucks its juices.

o. The Scorpion FLY (*Panorpa*). The male has an appendage on its tail, similar to the pincers of a scorpion.

p. (*Raphidia*); thorax elongated, forming a sort of neck.

q. The TERMITE (*Termes*), or White Ant. Its large wings are traversed by few veins. White Ants are found only in hot countries, where they are a scourge, because their larvæ make frightful havoc in wood-work, boring into beams, chests, &c. They live like ants, in large communities, of which there are four kinds: —

1. Winged males and their pupæ, with wing appendages.

2. Larger females, without wings.

3. Smaller larvæ, unprovided with wing appendages.

4. Sexless, unwinged ones, small and large, resembling larvæ, with large head. They do no work, but only defend the habitations; for which reason they are called soldiers.

The remarkable nests of these ants are built entirely of earth, about twelve feet high, and many together, which gives them the appearance of the villages of savages. Each building has an arched cupola on the top, which remains empty; only the lower part is inhabited; it contains the royal apartment, the habitations of the young ones, the private magazines or storehouses, and numberless passages. The arrangement of these buildings would do credit to the human understanding; and these works, gigantic in proportion to the size of the builders, are executed by insects of scarcely a quarter of an inch in length, and that in the space of from two to three years. The queen, of which there is only one in a community, has no other business than that of laying eggs, during which time the abdomen attains the length of three inches (see picture *q.*); she lays eggs continually, sometimes sixty in a minute, and more than eighty thousand within twenty-four hours. The Termites are eaten by several savage nations.

Plate 25.

IV. Bee, and Wasp-like Insects (*Hymenoptera*). — They have four membranous wings, more or less transparent; the hinder pair, the smaller. They have two upper jaws, horny, and fitted for biting or cutting; and two under jaws, longer and softer. The females have a piercer, or sting, in the hind extremity of the body.

a. The Gall Insect (*Cynips*). The female bores a hole in a plant, and deposits one or more eggs therein; the sap of the plant flows from the wound and forms an excrescence known by the name of gall-apple. The nut-gall, used in the preparation of ink, is formed in this manner upon the leaves of a species of oak, which grows in Asia Minor and in the East Indies. The Gall Insect bores rose-bushes as well as oaks.

Another species of Gall Insect lays its eggs in the fruit of the fig-tree, which renders the fruit not only much larger and sweeter, but causes it to ripen earlier.

b. The Golden Wasp (*Chrysis*) is of a brilliant, metallic color; it lays its eggs in the nests of mason and other bees, for which purpose it watches the favorable moment, when the mother has left the cell, that she may thrust her egg into it.

c. The Ichneumon Fly (*Ichneumon*). Its body is long and narrow; antennæ and legs, long. The female lays her eggs in the caterpillar, or pupa, of other insects. Though hidden in the most secret places, the Ichneumon finds them, and deposits one or more eggs in their body. These latter develop quickly, and nourish themselves from the fat body of the larva, gradually consuming its life; thus the Ichneumon destroys a great number of injurious caterpillars.

d. The Saw FLY (*Tenthredo*); body elongated, nearly cylindrical. Its larva has eighteen to twenty-two legs. The female bores holes into the twigs and other parts of plants, and lays in each an egg; in this way, they do much injury, as the larvæ eat away the tender sprouts of the plants.

e. The Earth BEE (*Sphex figulus*) makes a hole in the earth in which to lay its egg; is careful to put the body of an insect into the hole to nourish the pupa when developed, and then walls it up with clay.

f. The Mason BEE (*Eumenes muraria*). They make their habitations, which consist of four to twelve cells, running into each other, of sand and clay, and in each cell they lay an egg.

g. The WASP (*Vespa*). The Wasp, with its smooth, black and yellow body, is well known. Wasps live socially together; and their states, or colonies, are divided into males, females, and workers. The food of these Wasps is varied; they eat honey, fruit, sugar, wine, and meats; they kill bees and flies. Their nest is skilfully built; it is an oval, twelve to eighteen inches long, and ten to thirteen broad. It is too generally known to require farther description. The material of the building consists of a woody fibre, — which they gnaw from logs, &c., with their strong jaws, — moistened with a viscid secretion, and kneaded into a paste, resembling paper.

h. The Honey Bee (*Apis mellifica*). Bees are remarkable insects, which have attracted the attention of thinking people, on account of their artistic skill in building, their peculiar state constitution, and curious habits. In a natural state, they live in hollow trees; but when domesticated, they are put into hives. A community consists of males, or drones; females, or queens; and imperfect females, or workers. These differ in appearance, but still more in their manner of living. The community has but one queen, from eight hundred to a thousand males, and twenty to thirty thousand workers.

i. The Ant (*Formica*) is generally known. These insects, also, live in communities, consisting of males, females, and workers; the first are winged, and live only a few weeks; the latter are the chief population of the nest, and do all the labor. Although they do not build as artistically as bees, yet their activity and foresight are given as examples of diligence and industry.

V. Hemiptera. — The Hemiptera generally have wing-covers; a slender, horny beak, consisting of a horny sheath, in which are three stiff and sharp bristles, with which they suck the juices of plants and the blood of animals. They do not undergo a complete transformation. There are species in which the females, others in which both sexes, are wingless.

j. The Bedbug (*Acanthia (Cimex) lectularia*) is too well known to need description. It is not confined to houses, but is found in the pine forests of both hemispheres.

k. The Berry Bug (*Pentatoma baccarum*) is found on garden fruits and berries, and is known by its bad odor.

l. The Lantern Bearer (*Fulgora laternaria*). The Great American Lantern Bearer is an ornament to every collection of insects.

m. The Plant Louse (*Aphis*). The males are winged, the females wingless; they are small insects which live socially on plants. During the summer, they bring forth whole generations of female young; but the males come forth in the fall. They are injurious to the plants on which they live.

n. The Cochineal (*Coccus cacti*). The male has from two to four wings, but no beak; the females have no wings, but are provided with beaks. When they have laid their eggs, the body dries up, and serves as a covering to the eggs. From several kinds, a beautiful red color is produced; the most valuable is the real Cochineal of Mexico, which is cared for like the Silkworm, as it furnishes the most valuable carmine and scarlet colors.

VI. Butterflies (*Lepidoptera*). — Butterflies have six legs; a tongue, consisting of two tubular threads joined together so as to form a channel well adapted for suction; their wings, four in number, are covered on both sides with colored scales. They undergo a complete transformation.

A. Daily (*Diurna*). — The caterpillar is generally spiny or hairy, the chrysalis naked; and the Butterfly flies only in daytime. In tropical countries, there are beautifully colored butterflies, some of which are as large as a man's hand.

a. The Apollo Butterfly (*Parnassius Apollo*); wings, yellowish-white; the hind ones have red eye-spots. The larva is a velvety black, ornamented with red spots, and is found in mountainous countries.

b. The SWALLOW-TAIL (*Æronauta machaon*); beautiful yellow, with black trimmings, and blue and yellow crescent spots, bordered with black. In the caterpillar state, it feeds on fennel, carrots, &c.; it is green, with black cross-bands, and hairless.

c. The Camberwell BEAUTY, or White-bordered MANTLE (*Vanessa antiopa*); black, surrounded with blue spots, and bordered with yellow. To this species belongs also—

d. The ADMIRAL (*V. atlanta*); black wings, with a red band across the middle of the forward ones, and white spots near their tips; hind wings bordered with red. In the caterpillar state, it feeds upon nettles.

e. The Silver-washed FRITILLARY (*Argynnis paphia*). The hind wings are generally marked beneath with silvery or pearly spots. As a caterpillar, it feeds on violets.

f. The Purple Emperor BUTTERFLY (*Apatura iris*). The color above changes to blue; it has white bands. In the caterpillar state, it feeds on the willow.

g. The Common Azure BUTTERFLY (*Lycæna chryseis*). Small as this Butterfly is, it rivals the larger kinds by the splendor of its wings, blue bordered with white.

PLATE 26.

a. The Hawthorn BUTTERFLY (*Pieris cratægi*) has yellowish-white wings, with black veins; it is the caterpillar of this butterfly, which eats away the leaves of fruit-trees.

b. The Common Cabbage BUTTERFLY (*P. brassicæ*); upper wings, white, veined and bordered with black;

hind wings, yellow. In the caterpillar state, it feeds on cabbages.

B. EVENING MOTHS (*Crepuscularia*). — These Moths have the antennæ thickened in the middle, and more or less tapering at the ends; when at rest, the wings lie horizontally. They fly in the morning and evening twilight. The caterpillars are large, and have sixteen legs. The chrysalis is spherical, and generally enclosed in a cocoon made of a silky material.

c. The Humming-bird Hawk MOTH (*Sphynx* (*Macroglossa*) *stella*); antennæ running out to a point. This Moth flies rapidly, and makes a humming sound.

d. The Spotted Elephant Hawk Moth, or Spurge Sphinx (*Sphynx euphorbiæ*); wings, yellowish-brown, with beautiful green bands. The dark-green caterpillar lives on the cypress.

e. The Death's Head Hawk MOTH (*Acherontia atropos*); so called from the picture of a skull upon its back. It is a large Moth; seeks honey in beehives. The large yellow and blue striped caterpillar lives on potato-tops, lilacs, and flax.

f. The Eyed Hawk MOTH (*Smerinthus ocellatus*) is fawn-colored, clouded with brown on the front wings; hind wings, rose-colored, with a dark-blue eye surrounded by black, and having a black point in the middle. The bluish-green white striped caterpillar feeds on poplar and apple trees; this genus has a stout thorn on the tail.

g. The Bee Hawk MOTH (*Sesia*); antennæ compressed toward the end; the greater part of the surface of the front wing, transparent and glossy; hind wing, hairy. The caterpillar has no thorn. This Moth resembles a wasp, flies quickly, and makes a humming noise. The caterpillar lives in the interior of plants, and undergoes its transformation in its habitation.

h. The Spotted Burnet MOTH (*Zygæna filipendulæ*). The male has dark-blue, the female green, wings, with red spots. The caterpillar feeds on clover and soft grasses.

i. The Hop MOTH (*Hepiolus humuli*) in a caterpillar state gnaws the roots of hop-plants, and destroys them. The female of this Moth is yellowish, with orange stripes; the male is silver-colored.

C. NIGHT MOTHS (*Nocturna*). — These Moths have the antennæ long and tapering; wings, when at rest, lying horizontally, or rolled on the body. The caterpillars prepare a cocoon for their chrysalis state. These Moths fly in summer evenings after sundown. To this division belongs the genus *Bombyx*, with comb-like, or feathered antennæ. The larvæ have tubercles tipped with bristles, and have sixteen feet. They are distinguished from other caterpillars by their locomotions; the middle feet being wanting, it steps first with its fore feet, bends its body, and draws the hind feet forward, then stretches out the body, making rapid strides.

j. The Nocturnal PEACOCK'S EYE, or Emperor MOTH (*Bombyx pavonia*). This large Moth expands from five and a half to six inches; on each of its fine grayish-brown wings is a large eye-like spot. In the caterpillar state, it is green, with blue warts.

k. The Silkworm MOTH (*Bombyx mori*) has a large body, and dingy-white scalloped wings. Silk is made from the cocoon of the caterpillar. It feeds upon the leaves of the mulberry, and lives from six to seven weeks. Silk was brought into Europe from Asia in the year 1300. The cocoon contains about one thousand feet of silk.

l. The Black ARCHES (*Liparis monacha*) is whitish, with black zigzag lines. The caterpillar, with gray and blue warts, does much injury to pine forests.

m. The Goat MOTH (*Cossus ligniperda*) is found in the interior of oak, willow, and elm trees, which they hollow out with their strong jaws. It is of a beautiful red, with black head, and requires two years for its transformation. It is very injurious.

n. The Night Owl MOTH (*Noctua*); antennæ, simple; the upper wings differently colored from the lower ones. The caterpillar has sixteen feet.

o. The Clifden NONPAREIL (*Catocala fraxini*); a large and beautiful Moth, whose hinder wings have a blue cross-band on a black ground. The caterpillar lives on ash-trees.

p. The Lilac MOTH (*Phalæna syringaria*) has pointed wings, banded in different colors. The caterpillar lives on trees, and is distinguished from other caterpillars by having no legs in the middle of the body, so that, when it puts down its front legs, the body is curved, and the hind legs drawn forward, as if it intended to measure the space over which it moves; hence, called span-worms.

q. The Oak MOTH (*Tortrix quercus*); fore wings, green, with white cross-lines; hind wings, white.

PLUMED MOTHS (*Pterophorus*). — Wings divided by feathered segments.

r. The Many-plumed MOTH (*P. pentadactylus*); wings, snow-white; the upper divided into two, the under into three, feather-like parts; the caterpillar lives on plum and prune trees.

s. The Clothes MOTH (*Tinea sarcitella*) does great injury to woollen clothes.

t. The Fur MOTH (*T. pellionella*). The caterpillar is hatched in about fifteen days; it feeds on fur.

u. The Corn MOTH (*T. granella*) is known in the larva state as the white Corn-worm; it is very injurious to grain.

PLATE 27.

VII. DIPTERA, TWO-WINGED INSECTS. — These insects have two wings, six feet, and a mouth furnished with a sucker, or proboscis; the larva is a maggot; the pupa generally lies immovable in the dried skin of the larva.

a. The HORSE-FLY (*Œstrus*) is very large and thickly haired; proboscis hidden. They are the torment of horses, cows, &c., because they deposit their eggs upon them; and the larvæ, when hatched, suck their blood. The larvæ are under the skin, in the nostrils, the stomach, and the intestines.

b. The Hessian FLY (*Tabanus*); proboscis elongated; the head as large as the thorax; the eyes so large that they nearly touch each other. They suck the blood of men and animals, particularly that of horses and cattle.

c. The Stinging FLY (*Conops*) resembles the domestic fly, but stings badly.

d. The House FLY (*Musca domestica*). This importunate insect is everywhere, where man is; its larvæ are found in manure.

e. The Carrion Fly (*M. carnaria*) deposits its eggs, known as fly-blows, upon meat.

f. The Singing Gnat, or Mosquito (*Culex pipiens*). The females are the stingers; the males dance peaceably to their own music.

g. The Common Gnat (*Tipula*) is much larger than the Mosquito. The larvæ of this fly live in the ground, crawl in regular lines by thousands, and do much injury to the roots of plants.

VIII. Aptera, Wingless Insects.—These insects have six legs, and no wings; very few of them undergo metamorphoses.

h. The Louse (*Pediculus*). These disgusting insects are found upon man and beast.

i. The Flea (*Pulex irritans*). These little creatures, known over all the world, are always wide-awake; a great annoyance to animals and man.

j. The Sand Flea (*P. penetrans*) is much more dangerous than the preceding; it is common in South America and the East Indies. It bores under men's toe-nails, where it deposits its eggs. If not cut out in season, the maggots produce a dangerous swelling, and the amputation of the part becomes necessary. Called chigoe and jigger.

k. The Centipede (*Scolopendra*) has many feet; the body is long, composed of many rings, each of which has a pair of feet. It feeds on insects. The stinging Centipede has twenty-one pairs of feet, and attains a length of five inches; it is found in the West Indies. Its bite is very poisonous.

IX. Arachnida, or Spiders.—These are articulated, and without antennæ or wings; they have the head and thorax united into one piece.

l. The WOODTICK (*Ixotes ricinus*); body, leathery; eyes, indistinct. Woodticks live on trees and grasses, from which they fall upon cattle and sheep, penetrating under their skin, so that they must be cut out to relieve the animal.

m. The MITE (*Acarus*) has a soft body, and jaws like nippers; most of them are so small as to be seen only through a microscope. Mites live upon various articles of food, the skin of animals, sores, &c.; they are common everywhere.

ARANEA, OR COMMON SPIDERS. — Of these there are many kinds which spin their artistic tissues, partly as dwellings and nets for catching food, and partly as a covering for their eggs. All live on smaller animals, or eat each other; even the females eat the males.

n. The Tortoise Shell SPIDER (*Aranea diadema*).

o. The Domestic, or House SPIDER (*A. domestica*).

p. The TARANTULA (*Lycosa tarantula*). The bite of this Spider is less dangerous than is reported. It is common in the torrid zone.

q. The SCORPION (*Scorpio*). Thorax and abdomen transversely. Its long, segmented tail ends in a sting, from the point of which flows a poison. The sting of the larger kinds of Scorpions is very dangerous in hot climates. They live on insects, and are viviparous.

r. The Book SCORPION (*Chelifer cancroides*) is small, and is found in books.

CRABS AND LOBSTERS. — Head and thorax more or less covered with a hard carapace, or coat-of-mail; the mouth provided with complete jaws. They undergo no metamorphosis, and are the most perfect animals of this class. There are a great many species, particularly in the sea.

t. Common River CRAB, or CRAYFISH (*Astacus fluviatilis*). Its color is sometimes light, sometimes dark; when cooked, it is red. The tail of a dead Crab stands out straight. Crabs live to a great age, sometimes twenty years, and become very large. This Crab is less eaten in the summer than at other seasons.

u. The LOBSTER (*A. (Homarus) marinus*) is about one and a half feet long; a valuable article of food.

v. The Land CRAB (*Gecarcinus ruricola*) is found in South America and the West Indies; it lives the greater part of the year on land, where it hides itself in holes in the earth, during the day, and comes out toward evening to seek food; it runs quickly. At the time of breeding, these Crabs go, in immense crowds, to the sea to lay their eggs. Many are caught, and they are highly esteemed as savory food.

w. The Hermit CRAB (*Pagurus bernhardi*) has a naked tail, which it thrusts into empty shells, to preserve it from harm. It is common.

x. The Cellar Wood LOUSE (*Oniscus asellus*). The tail has six segments. The Wood Louse lives in dark and damp places. Called also Sow Bug or Pill Bug.

y. The Molucca KING, or Horseshoe CRAB (*Limulus*) inhabits the Indian Ocean; is from one to two feet long, and moves slowly. There are species in America.

z. The Water FLEA (*Daphnia pulex*); the body covered by a transparent shell; the head separated; feet, like branches. These animals are small; red in spring and summer, and at other times a greenish-white. They are found in great numbers in stagnant waters, in which they swim quickly. To these belong, also, *a. b.* and *d.* of Plate 20.

Plate 28.

Worms (*Vermes*). — Worms have a long body, more or less cylindrical, and composed of rings or segments. They either have no feet, or the feet are not articulate.

Among the intestinal Worms (*Entozoa*), those which live in the intestines of larger animals, are the following: —

a. The Hydatid (*Cysticercus*). These worms live in the brain and liver of animals, causing fatal diseases.

b. The Ascaris (*Ascaris vermicularis et lumbricoides*) is frequently in the intestines of man, particularly of children. Some are small and thread-like, called pinworms; others are thick, like earth-worms.

c. The Thread, or Guinea, Worm (*Filaria medinensis*) is about twelve feet long, and no larger than a thread. It is common in tropical climates, particularly in Asia and Africa, where it is found under the skin of man, usually that of the feet; it must be wound out from the flesh with the greatest care, as mortification often takes place where the worm is broken.

d. The Tape Worm (*Tænia*) is flat, like a ribbon; the body consists of many segments; the front part of the worm is thin and narrow, and widens toward the tail. The head is hardly discernible to the naked eye. The Tape Worm lives in man's intestines, is often from twenty to twenty-four feet long, and longer. It is very troublesome, and removed from the body with much difficulty.

Annularia. — These worms have a circulation of

red blood; no visible external organs of respiration, but appear to respire by the entire surface.

e. The Earth WORM (*Lumbricus terrestris*) is about six inches long, and composed of more than one hundred rings. It lives in moist, rich soils, gnaws at the small roots of garden plants and destroys them.

HIRUDO. — The LEECH. The mouth of the Leech is armed with three jaws and encircled with a lip; the hind extremity with a flattened disk, well adapted to adhere to other bodies. All the species of Leech live in water, and will suck blood.

f. The Medical LEECH (*Hirudo officinalis*); back, black, with six longitudinal red bands; belly, olive-yellow. Leeches are used for bleeding, and form an important article of commerce.

g. The Horse LEECH (*H. galo*) is of a darker color, and without dorsal bands. It cannot be used, as its bite causes severe wounds.

TUBICOLÆ. — Worms living in shelly tubes.

h. The TOOTHSHELL (*Dentalium*). The shell tube is open at both ends.

i. The WORMSHELL (*Serpula*). The worm inhabits a hard, calcareous, round tube; the branchiæ look like feathers.

k. The NEREID (*Nereis*). These worms stand upright in sea-sand; many of them shed a phosphoric light.

l. The FELTWORM (*Aphrodita*). The strong thorns, and tufts of fine bristles which protrude from its sides, have the lustre of gold; and, in splendor of color, they are not inferior to precious stones and humming-birds.

m. The NAIDWORM (*Nais*) has a transparent body, bordered with bristles; found, usually, in fresh waters.

RADIATA.—Radiates. The characteristic of these animals is their ray-like form. Their chief organs lie in the middle, the others surround them like rays; most of them have a mouth and a tube for digestion; head, and organs of sense, wanting; nerves are also wanting in the most of them. They differ greatly in their exterior form; all live in the water.

n. The Green Polyp (*Hydra viridis*) attains the length of half a foot; the arms are shorter than the body. This small animal resembles an animated plant.

There are numerous plant-like animals in the sea, with tentacules, or arms; they live together in great numbers. From their bodies, they secrete a hard, solid, horny, or stone-like mass; such societies, with their trunk, are called zoöphytes, or animal plants; among them are reckoned —

o. The SEA-CORK (*Alcyonium*) becomes cork-like when dry, and is brittle: when fresh, it is fleshy and pliable, and is entirely composed of small polyps.

We have also illustrated the common sponge (*Spongia marina*), which has been until now counted among the armed polyps, and which decidedly belongs to animal plants. It is mostly found around the islands, and in the bays of the Mediterranean, and is brought up from the depth of the sea by divers. In the fresh state, the holes of the sponge are filled with organic and gelatinous matter, from which it must be cleaned to preserve it.

Plate 29.

a. The Horn Coral (*Gorgonia*); the trunk, smooth, horny, and sometimes woody; the fleshy bark does not fall off when taken out of the water, but remains as a calcareous covering. Many kinds of these beautiful Corals are found in all seas.

b. The Sea-feather (*Pennatula*). The trunk is a simple hollow stalk, naked below, and adorned with thousands of polyps above. All polyps, like the Sea-feather, are moved by one will, as they move at once, and in the same direction.

c. The Millepores (*Millepora*); trunk, naked, or branching, with minute openings; the polyps generally without arms.

d. The Star-coral (*Madrepora*). They have beautiful star-like openings.

These Corals grow quickly, and are known under the name of coral reefs and coral banks, and become dangerous to navigation. Sometimes they rise above the surface of the water, and form entire islands, whose surface, in process of time, serves for the habitation of man.

e. The Red Coral (*Isis nobilis*) is generally at the bottom of the sea, where it stands like a stone tree. It is brought up by divers and by nets; beautiful necklaces and other ornaments are made of it.

Jelly-fishes (*Acalephæ*) are gelatinous, free-swimming Radiates, provided with radiating tubes for digestion. They are found in all seas; they shine during the night. Their tentacles produce a kind of stinging, by which they immediately kill small animals, to carry them to their mouth.

f. The Rose JELLY-FISH (*Medusa rosea*) is found in the Baltic.

g. The Common JELLY-FISH, Sea-blubber (*Velella*); having a flat cartilage on the upper part, which the animal uses for a sail when swimming. It is brilliant at night, everywhere common.

h. The Ribbed JELLY-FISH (*Beroë*); body, round, or oval, ornamented with eight rows of locomotive appendages. The most of them give a brilliant light, and sparkle like precious stones.

i. The Portuguese MAN-OF-WAR (*Physalia Stephanonia*) consists of a crested air sac, which floats lightly upon the water; under its surface are numerous long and varied appendages. It is about eight inches long, and beautifully colored; found in the Atlantic Ocean.

k. The GIRDLE OF VENUS (*Stephanonia Amphitritis*) is also found in the Atlantic; it shines by night like a crown of stars.

PLATE 30.

a. The Marine NETTLE, sea anemone, animal flower (*Actinia*), resembles a colored flower, with many leaves, which rests firmly on a broad smooth body.

The Echinoderms, Star-fishes, and Sea Urchins are more perfectly organized than the Acalephs.

b. The Common STAR-FISH (*Asterias*) is formed, like a star, with five rays.

c. The Snake STAR-FISH (*Ophiura*) forms a disk, from which grow out five long, articulated rays, in the form of serpents; common to all seas.

d. The Sea URCHIN (*Echinus*); round, with a thin calcareous shell, which has a large mouth, with five strong teeth on the under side. On the outside of the shell are regular, long rows of warts, from which project spines, movable at the will of the animal. The eggs are situated at the anus, and pass out through a particular opening. The Sea Urchin is found in all seas, and is eaten by many people.

e. The MEDUSA (*Gorgonocephalus*). The body has five rays, which can be subdivided to infinity. It is found in all seas.

f. The Sea LILY (*Pentacrinus*); stalk, five-sided; star with five rays, and these are again subdivided. Each part can move independently of the other parts. It is found in the waters of the West Indies. It is the only living representative of the ancient crinoids, or stone-lilies, so abundant in the palæozoic rocks.

www.ingramcontent.com/pod-product-compliance
Lightning Source LLC
Chambersburg PA
CBHW030243170426
43202CB00009B/609